Mercedes-Benz
M-CLASS

BY JOHN LAMM

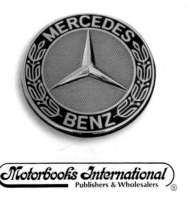

Motorbooks International
Publishers & Wholesalers ®

CONTENTS

FOREWORD 5

Chapter 1: Introduction
TURNAROUND 20

Chapter 2: The Sport-Utility Market
FROM G-WAGEN TO M-CLASS.....................28

Chapter 3: Where to Build the M-Class
WHERE IN THE WORLD? 36

Chapter 4: Styling
SKETCHES, CLAY & METAL........................46

Chapter 5: Safety & Engineering
LIVING PROOF 62

Chapter 6: The All-New V-6 & V-8 Engines
THE HEART OF THE MATTER 76

Chapter 7: The 4wd System
COMING TO GRIPS............................84

Chapter 8: Development Trips
CAMELS & FROZEN LAKES........................96

Chapter 9: The Learning Field
NEW FACTORY, NEW METHODS 106

Chapter 10: Manufacturing
OPERATING ON THE EDGE 118

Chapter 11: The Human Side
PEOPLE POWER 136

Chapter 12: Behind the Wheel
A WORLD-CLASS PERFORMER.....................144

Chapter 13: The Lost World: Jurassic Park
MOVIE STAR 152

Chapter 14: Andreas Renschler, President and CEO, MBUSI
THE M TEAM 158

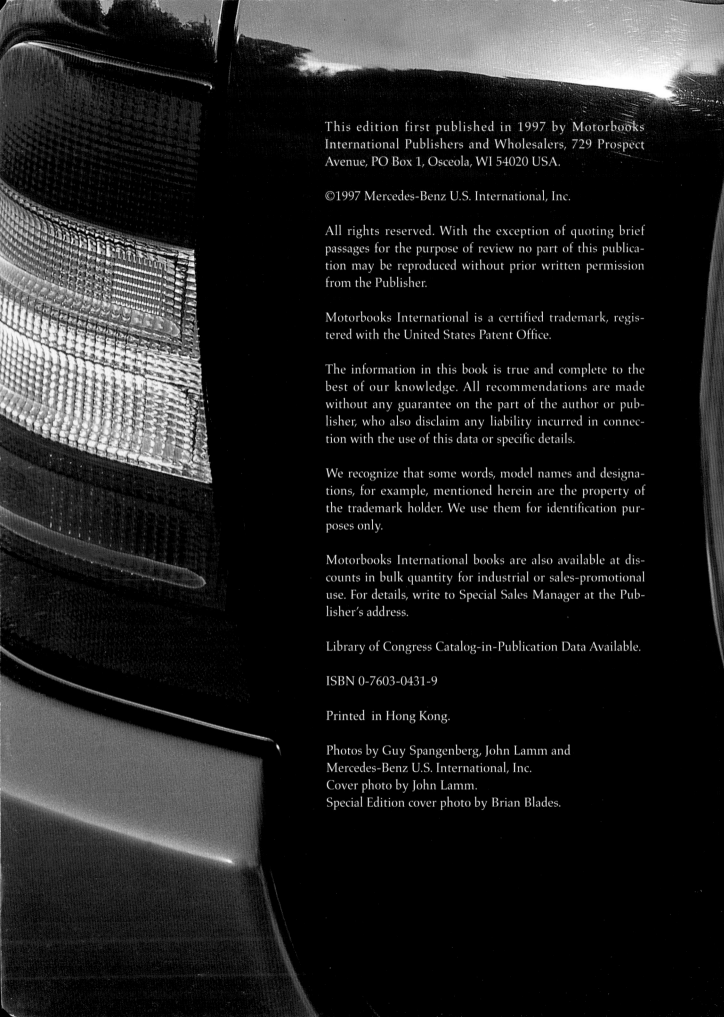

This edition first published in 1997 by Motorbooks International Publishers and Wholesalers, 729 Prospect Avenue, PO Box 1, Osceola, WI 54020 USA.

©1997 Mercedes-Benz U.S. International, Inc.

Motorbooks International books are also available at discounts in bulk quantity for industrial or sales-promotional use. For details, write to Special Sales Manager at the Publisher's address.

Library of Congress Catalog-in-Publication Data Available.

ISBN 0-7603-0431-9

Printed in Hong Kong.

Photos by Guy Spangenberg, John Lamm and Mercedes-Benz U.S. International, Inc.
Cover photo by John Lamm.
Special Edition cover photo by Brian Blades.

FOREWORD

It began less than five years ago as just an idea—a vision of a new way of operating, a vision of a new vehicle worthy of the renowned three-pointed star. Today, we welcome the M-Class as the youngest member of our family, a true Mercedes made by Daimler-Benz. This new vehicle is the latest chapter in the 110-year autobiography of the world's oldest automaker, and it can tell many fascinating stories.

The Mercedes-Benz M-Class story is not only about a new type of automobile. It is a story about change—change in the way our company looks at itself, change in the way we do things. It is also a story about people—people from different cultures and with different experiences, working together. And, of course, it is a story about a new vehicle that will set a new standard among sport utilities.

The M-Class story is also a living example of the Daimler-Benz globalization strategy. But when you read this book and relive the M-Class story, you will realize that globalization is not just about expanding one's business, or setting up new production facilities abroad, or gaining a competitive advantage. It's also about bringing together different people, ideas and cultures, in an effort to establish new ways of working and better means of serving our customers.

The M-Class team took on a tremendous challenge: establishing a new plant in a new country, building a new product with a new team of individuals. No easy task, yet one which can only be accomplished with a determination and a spirit that comes when you believe in your product and you work as a team. And this is what impressed me most about the people behind the M-Class—they truly are a team.

I commend all of the people who helped to make the Mercedes-Benz M-Class come to life. Likewise, I applaud the many others in our company who have helped the M-Class team achieve what they have during the past four years.

And a special thanks to the fine people of the State of Alabama, whom we are proud to have as our neighbors and friends.

Enjoy our story

Yours sincerely

JÜRGEN SCHREMPP
Chairman, Daimler-Benz AG

Presenting the newest
Mercedes-Benz...
THE M-CLASS.
A luxurious sport-utility
vehicle that features
world-class engineering,
a unique 4-wheel-drive
system and car-like ride
and handling character.
The M-Class is built at
a new factory in Alabama,
showcasing Daimler-Benz's
globalization plans.

① Introduction

TURN-AROUND

As the new millennium approaches, Mercedes-Benz has to take a hard look back across its 100-year history and decide if it can continue to do business in the traditional manner. Germany is unified and new markets begin to emerge on all the world's continents. It's a time of tough choices and history-making decisions.

It begins, of course, with Karl Benz and Gottlieb Daimler. Make no mistake about that. This story of the late Nineties draws a direct line back over 100 years to the men given credit for creating the first automobiles and what would prove to be the foundation of Mercedes-Benz.

Their world was one of hot-tube ignition, horizontal flywheels and the amazing thought of removing the horse from the transportation equation. Today we consider fuel injection, microprocessors and the ground-breaking idea of building a Mercedes-Benz outside of Germany. In

The Benz "Patent-Motorwagen" of 1886 is hailed as the world's first internal-combustion-powered automobile, ushering in the era of the horseless carriage. Also note what is possibly the world's first car advertisement.

1888, Bertha Benz and her sons made history by driving 50 miles from Mannheim to Pforzheim, buying fuel for their single-cylinder horseless carriage at pharmacies. At the start of the 21st century, you'll easily make that distance in a full-time 4-wheel-drive Mercedes-Benz M-Class before you are halfway through one musical CD and your fuel-level needle has barely moved. All part of the continuing history begun by Daimler and Benz.

The timeline is well chronicled. Daimler and Benz expanded their small companies in the 1890s, developing their horseless carriages into ever-more practical automobiles. Daimler named his advanced 1901 model "Mercedes," adding that name to the automotive lexicon. Rac-

ing helped prove the worth of the automobile in the century's first two decades and did much to aid its development, and among two of the most famous were Benz's 1908 and the Mercedes 1914 Grand Prix cars.

Paralleling the racing efforts was an expanding line of production cars from the two companies. In both cases total production wasn't that high, but the quality was, making both Mercedes and Benz the sorts of automobiles preferred by wealthy, discriminating buyers. Daimler and Benz merged in 1926 and by the early Thirties had an extensive model range crowned by famous automobiles such as the SSK and the 540K. At the same time, their racing cars were setting records throughout Europe.

Rebuilding a war-shattered company at great speed in the Fifties, Mercedes-Benz produced such modern classics as the 300SL and 300S, while also cre-

A Karl Benz. **B** Gottlieb Daimler in the first motorcar of his design, driven by his son, 1886. **C** A mechanic takes a careful look at the tire of this 1908 Mercedes Grand Prix car. **D** 1922 Mercedes Targa Florio. **E** 1929 Mercedes-Benz SSK. **F** The magnificent, straight-8 supercharged Mercedes 540K. **G** 1953 Mercedes-Benz 300S Coupe. **H** 1958 Mercedes-Benz 300SL.

ating another genera-
tion of race cars that
became their genera-
tion's competition
benchmark. And as
the century worked
through its final
decades, the name
Mercedes-Benz be-
came the best-known
automotive brand in the world. It
earned a reputation as the car you aspire
to own, whether it be a solid sedan, an SL
sports car or an almost regal, top-of-the-
line S model.

Just as surely as Karl Benz and Gottlieb
Daimler had the vision to see that they
could dramatically change the manner in
which men moved across the
world, the men at Mercedes-Benz
100 years later watched as their
world changed dramatically, and
made plans for the company to
change along with it.

Helmut Werner, the chairman
of Mercedes-Benz during those
years, explains: "We had a glori-
ous decade in the Seventies. In

23

the Eighties we harvested from all the achievements of the Seventies, but we did not really generate enough new ideas to cope with the challenges of the Eighties and Nineties. That became very obvious in the last years of the Eighties, and it was, of course, emphasized by the facts and the consequences of the fall of the Berlin Wall and the reunification of Germany. The world became much more open and that had a big impact on how our customers envisioned cars and how best to use them. We had to learn that lesson and we had to be pretty quick on our feet."

Jürgen Hubbert, Mercedes-Benz board member for passenger cars, echoes Werner's thoughts when he adds, "I think that in order to understand the changes in our strategy we have to see that we had this long history, 40 years of success. When we found ourselves in this position in the mid-Eighties, we saw that we had some weaknesses and we understood that our competitors were willing to take advantage of these weaknesses. Therefore, we formed a strategy to bring Mercedes back on the road to success."

Critics were uncertain if Mercedes-Benz could accomplish this "turnaround" with the necessary speed. The very things that had made the company great—its history, its automobiles, its culture—also might have created a momentum that would make it difficult to easily redirect the company before the end of the century.

Mercedes' management board thought otherwise. And though it wouldn't be easy, the board set the company on a new course. Hubbert admits, "It is very difficult to turn around in such a short time…and to do this you need three things: a vision, a strategy and a very motivated team. The vision was quite clear. We said we wanted to be number one in profitability and innovation by the year 2000 at the latest.

"That's why we decided on four offenses: one for products, one for productivity, one for globalization and one for learning. We presented this to our staff and immediately everyone understood that we had to make these changes to be more competitive in the future. I think we also needed the crisis in the market in the years 1992–1993 so everyone understood that the so-called 'good old times' would never come back."

Instead of reeling under the weight of its history and momentum, Mercedes decided to turn this force to its advantage. Says Helmut Werner: "We have a very rich history that has been built up over the past 100 years, and everybody around the globe knows what Mercedes is today. This offers an ideal platform for the future development of the company. We just have to utilize it correctly. We have to transform it into something that our customers will ac-

cept, both today and tomorrow.

"We started work on that transformation in the Eighties, having slightly reoriented the direction of the three-pointed star and given it a somewhat new definition. In our opinion, this new direction very much fits modern market needs and will enable us to exploit modern market potentials. So we use that long history as a starting place to find a combination of the good old features, traditions and habits and bring it into a new exciting formula that will be of high interest for our customers."

That exciting formula meant a list of new products, and with surprising speed the changes began. For decades, introductions of new Mercedes models were so infrequent and product life cycles so long that the company's public relations department had plenty of time to deal with each launch individually. Now the steady stream of new offerings has the press department working overtime as new vehicles are introduced.

Several models, such as the C-Class and E-Class, were dramatically revised versions of older models, the latter causing a stir with a switch back to round headlights. This pair was joined by products aimed at market segments the company had historically avoided: the A-Class city car, the V-Class van, the small C-Class wagon and the SLK sports car, which is fitted with a clever folding steel top and aimed at a younger and less affluent audience than past Mercedes sports cars.

Although Mercedes enjoyed (and continues to enjoy) a tremendous reputation throughout the world, its new strategy meant it would have to change where and how it would sell all these new products. Mercedes knew it had to face the fact that there is limited growth potential in the traditional markets…the United States, Europe and also Japan. Therefore, it had to look to new emerging markets whose customers represent a tremendous potential for Mercedes-Benz.

Dieter Zetsche is the board member responsible for marketing Mercedes cars around the world, and he says the company also had to reconsider where its vehicles would be built. "For every company, including Mercedes, it's important to

I Mercedes-Benz Mountain Bike. **J** Smart Car concept by Mercedes-Benz. **K** The A-Class, a model of compact efficiency. **L** The C-Class, worthy successor to the 190E. **M** Mercedes-Benz C-Class wagon. **N** Mercedes-Benz SLK230: supercharged power, retractable hardtop ingenuity.

grow," he begins. "In the traditional markets the growth potential is limited so it's important to seek new markets everywhere. There are many countries in which tariff barriers alone won't allow you to enter merely by importing. You have to go there with your factories. There are other places where the customer feels greater closeness to a manufacturer if there is a plant in his country. Both arguments clearly call for a globalization strategy."

Jürgen Hubbert adds another reason for overseas production, explaining that, "The problems of currency brought us to the conclusion that we need to have more production outside Germany. When we started our offensive we had just 5 percent of our production outside Germany. When you look at the year 2000, we expect to have 25 percent in other countries. So that will result in this big change for Mercedes, from 'Made in Germany' to 'Made by Mercedes-Benz.'"

For years there have been Mercedes factories in some markets where automobiles are assembled with large pieces that are imported. Mercedes' new thinking, however, goes well beyond that. It calls

for creating complete factories overseas, some to build unique products that better suit that faraway market. To do that, Mercedes must export something more difficult than automobiles: culture. As that famous tag "Made in Germany" is being replaced with "Made by Mercedes-Benz," all the expected Mercedes traits, such as safety, quality and durability, must be included.

Helmut Werner feels such a transfer of corporate traits can be done easily because Mercedes has a tradition of doing that. The company started making trucks in Brazil in the middle of the Fifties and today nobody would claim that these trucks are of lesser quality compared to those built in Germany. With evidence that the quality of Mercedes can be upheld on the commercial vehicle side, it will certainly be repeated on the car side.

The United States is not a newly emerging market, of course, and more Mercedes-Benz cars are sold there than in any other country outside Germany. So as the company began to investigate potential factories beyond the traditional

borders, the U.S. was a logical candidate. And with sales of the quintessentially American sport-utility vehicle continuing to grow, a U.S.-based factory became an important part of Mercedes-Benz's new-model strategy.

Mercedes-Benz, however, turned its move to America into something much more than just an offshore factory building a new type of vehicle. This was to become a laboratory for methods and processes that would change how Mercedes would operate in the future…a new Mercedes-Benz that recently changed its motto from "Nothing but the best" to "Nothing but the best for our customers."

Jürgen Hubbert explains: "You know that even in the United States we said the Mercedes was, 'Engineered like no other car in the world.' That showed the cars

were designed and built to please engineers, and the customers were secondary. Today we say that our customers define the product…this is the man, the woman who wants to have the car, and this means that every technology, every system has to be developed and has to be customer oriented…that's the big change and I think we have been very successful with this change."

Which explains why this newest of Mercedes-Benz automobiles is a very American-style vehicle assembled in a factory where a short drive won't get you any *Sauerbraten* but will bring you to reputedly the best barbecued ribs in America. And while Tuscaloosa has no *Fussball* to speak of, it is home to the University of Alabama Crimson Tide, one of the great football dynasties in America. The result is an efficient and international factory in the land of the legendary Paul "Bear" Bryant.

O The CLK: a sporty new coupe. **P** Mercedes' newest family member, the M-Class sport utility. **Q** The bold look of the E-Class has its roots in M-B sedans of the Fifties. **R** The E-Class wagon. **S** The V-Class. **T** The go-anywhere G-Wagen, whose boxy styling is in marked contrast to the smooth contours of the M-Class. **U** The Bremen-built SL-Class. **V** The flagship S-Class.

FROM G-WAGEN TO M-CLASS

Mercedes-Benz already had a heavy-duty off-road vehicle, the famous Geländewagen. They could redesign the G-Wagen, but would that vehicle be consistent with Mercedes' new market-driven product line? If not, what sort of SUV should wear the Mercedes star?

It's one thing for a company to conceive of a new philosophy and to espouse a different way of doing business, but quite another to implement it. This was not a problem for Mercedes-Benz. During 1991 and into 1992, feasibility studies were made, delving into how to re-orient the three-pointed star. The fact that Andreas Renschler, then only 34, headed a major group says a great deal about how

A

head a project to decide if Mercedes should build a sport-utility vehicle, and where. That was in March, 1992, and then in October, Daimler's board approved the basic plan. The next few months of intense activity more clearly defined just what and where, and in April, 1993, Mercedes-Benz formally announced it would build a 4-wheel-drive sport-utility vehicle in North America.

much the 105-year-old company realized it needed to change.

Renschler, whose education includes degrees in economic engineering and business administration, was not bound by all the historical ties that can be as much help as hindrance to a firm such as Mercedes. Having started at Mercedes in 1988, he soon joined the Chairman of the Board of Management's staff and only a short while later became the assistant to the soon-to-be chairman, Helmut Werner. Involved in the turnaround turmoil from the start, Renschler was named by Prof. Neifer to

And because Andreas Renschler had been so persuasive in his arguments, the honor of carrying the project—new vehicle, new factory, new country, a new way of doing business—fell into his hands… an honor that was also a staggering responsibility.

From the start, this new built-in-America Mercedes-Benz was called the All-Activity Vehicle. Following the company's standard procedure for naming vehicles, it later officially was called the M-Class. But it won't be the first Mercedes built in the U.S. That honor goes to the piano-making Steinways, who in 1905 produced their first passenger cars. In a factory on Long Island, New York, Steinway made fewer than 100 American Mercedes based on plans and many

B

parts supplied from Germany. Alas, in 1907 a fire destroyed the factory and the $500,000 needed to restart the project was just too much. Only one or two American Mercedes still exist, with a fine example owned by Mercedes-Benz of North America. Who is to say what might have happened if the factory hadn't burned?

Ninety years later, there will again be an American-built Mercedes passenger vehicle, and again it will contain certain German-made parts. But this time it will not be a luxury automobile aimed at the most exclusive of clients. In the early 1900s, listening to the customer meant individual orders, choosing a wheelbase and a body type, and possibly even hiring a man to drive the car. These days listening to the voice of the customer has a much different meaning, and what those voices are loudly demanding are sport-utility vehicles, which are commonly known as SUVs.

Sport-utility vehicles are not a purely American phenomenon, as witnessed by years of Land Rovers, Toyota Land Cruisers and Nissan Patrols, but the U.S., with its wide open spaces and cheap gasoline, has become the homeland for the market.

It's difficult to pin down just what was the first sport-utility vehicle. Before World War II there was a rather definitive line drawn between automobiles and commercial vehicles. Hoping to find a civilian market for its rugged Jeep, Willys-Overland produced a 4-wheel-drive station wagon soon after the war ended. These boxy and rather homely bodies matched to the classic Jeep face might be the originals, but they were cer-

tainly more utilitarian than sporty. This generation of staid and hefty machines was developed over the years with ever-increasing comfort, leading to the 1963 debut of the Jeep Wagoneer. Offered with two or four doors and with 2- or 4-wheel drive, these Jeeps are the real grandfathers of the current sport-utility craze. The price for a 1963 4-door, 4-wheel-drive Wagoneer powered by a 6-cylinder engine was $3332.

While the Wagoneer might have started the modern sport-utility segment, its rise to prominence and popularity needed more excitement and pizazz than the big Jeep could provide. The "sport" side of sport utility received a boost starting with an odd machine, International Harvester's 1961 Scout. Detroit got on the bandwagon and installed real horsepower with the Ford Bronco (1966), Chevrolet Blazer (1968), GMC Jimmy (1970) and Dodge Ramcharger (1974). Broncos, Blazers and Ramchargers could be seen in off-road magazines and races, leaping off sand

A A partially disguised M-Class takes a breather alongside a G-Wagen at the same German military test site used to develop the latter. **B** The first American-built Mercedes, a 1905 model built largely from imported German parts by the piano-making Steinways. **C** The M-Class owes a nod of respect to what's considered the granddaddy of all sport-utes, the Jeep Wagoneer.

GROWTH OF THE SUV MARKET IN THE U.S., 1980-'96

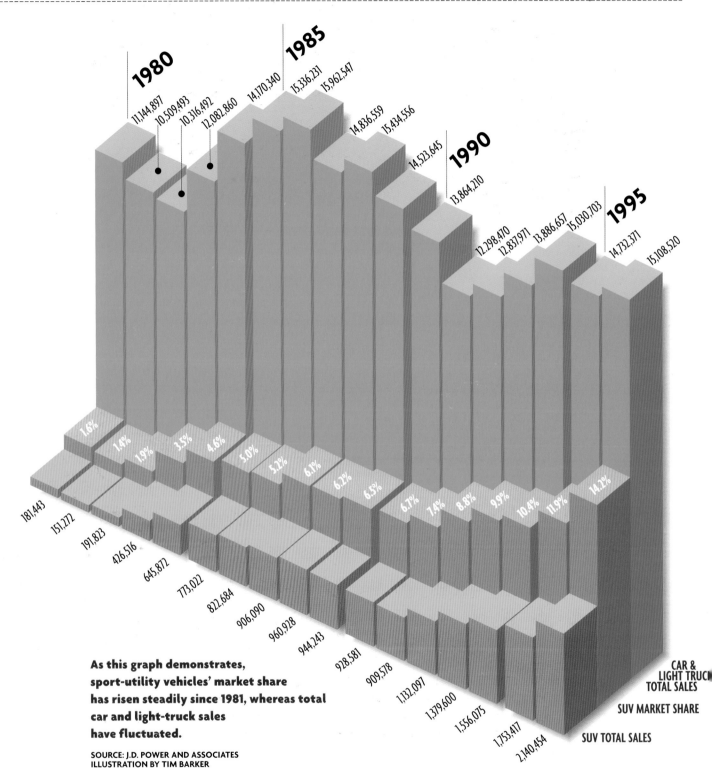

1980

11,144,897
10,509,493
10,316,492
12,082,860

1985

14,170,340
15,336,231
15,962,547
14,836,559
15,434,556
14,523,645
13,864,210

1990

12,298,470
12,837,971
13,886,657
15,030,703

1995

14,732,371
15,108,520

1.6%
1.4%
1.9%
3.5%
4.6%
5.0%
5.2%
6.1%
6.2%
6.5%
6.7%
7.4%
8.8%
9.9%
10.4%
11.9%
14.2%

181,443
151,272
191,823
426,516
645,872
773,022
822,684
906,090
960,928
944,243
928,581
909,578
1,132,097
1,379,600
1,556,075
1,753,417
2,140,454

CAR &
LIGHT TRUCK
TOTAL SALES

SUV MARKET SHARE

SUV TOTAL SALES

As this graph demonstrates,
sport-utility vehicles' market share
has risen steadily since 1981, whereas total
car and light-truck sales
have fluctuated.

SOURCE: J.D. POWER AND ASSOCIATES
ILLUSTRATION BY TIM BARKER

dunes or climbing steep hills. While few owners of current sport-utility machines would use their Jimmy, Explorer or Grand Cherokee to go off-road, this rough-and-tumble image created over the past 30 years remains an important part of the SUV purchase decision.

That's the buyer's view. The automaker's point of view is quite different and is measured in market share. In 1980, before the sport-utility movement skyrocketed, total sales in the U.S. were less than 200,000. The momentum began to build by the mid-Eighties and 10 years later SUVs continue to be the hottest growth segment of the new-car market.

You can see the results on every street in America, but here's how it comes out in hard numbers. In 1985, 773,022 SUVs were sold in the U.S. versus 14.5 million cars and light trucks. Those numbers meant that sport-utility vehicles then had captured 5 percent of the overall market. By the time all the sales were totaled for 1996, sport-utility-vehicle sales had almost tripled to a phenomenal 2.1 million or 14.2 percent of the market.

D Though originally developed for the military, the G-Wagen was later adapted for civilian use. Duly civilized, it's as classy at the country club as it is rugged off the road. **E** Mercedes' towering 8-ft-tall, 7-ton Unimog may well be the ultimate sport-utility vehicle—its imposing presence might even make an AM General Hummer feel a little insecure.

Such growth is simply amazing, and so is the variety of sport-utility machines. They continue to crop up in all shapes and sizes, and at every level from rugged simplicity to utmost luxury. They are built throughout the world, often with one model assuming various identities in different countries, such as the Isuzu Rodeo, which is also the Honda Passport in America and the Opel/Vauxhall Frontera in Europe. In Europe, one assembly line produces both the Nissan Terrano and the Ford Maverick. Sizes vary from the very small machines in Japan to the monstrous AM General Hummer in America. Names run the gamut and include Rocky, Levante, Rasheen, Galloper, Rugger, Magnum, Freeclimber and the Proceed Marvi.

Work your way through worldwide SUV production, and you find that one of the smaller outputs is a line in the Steyr-Daimler-Puch factory in Graz, Austria. In 1996, it produced close to 4700 Geländewagens or, more simply, G-Wagens. Other than the Unimog truck, this has been Mercedes-Benz's only entry in the sport-utility field.

Originally designed for military use, the G-Wagen is a wonder car for anyone with off-road aspirations because of its numerous desirable traits. Like being able to shift between high and low gear ranges in the transfer case while moving, or electronically locking the center, the rear and, finally, the front differential for the ultimate in traction. And because even an off-road Mercedes-Benz is still part of the family, the interior is nicely finished with the options of polished wood trim and leather upholstery.

With the fall of the Berlin Wall and the easing of East-West political tensions, the demand for military vehicles subsided

and Mercedes moved the G-Wagen's development team to the passenger-car division. With the decision to shift Mercedes' SUV emphasis more to the consumer side came the matter of which segment to target. Should the G-Wagen be significantly re-engineered and fight with the Toyota Land Cruiser and Range Rover for that narrow slice of the sport-utility pie filled with luxurious vehicles? Chances are it would have sold well. Besides, that's what would have been expected of the traditional Mercedes-Benz.

Or should Mercedes change its view of the SUV market? And how? After all, it was Mercedes chairman Helmut Werner who talked about changing the direction of the three-pointed star and giving it a somewhat new definition.

And that's precisely what Mercedes-Benz did, taking direct aim at the heart of the SUV market.

If the company had stayed with the G-Wagen and given it a modern updating, the price would have come in at $55,000–60,000, with estimated sales of 5000 per year in the U.S. By changing the aim of its sport-utility entry, Mercedes put the M-Class in the mid-$30,000 price range, which means that sales may exceed 40,000 vehicles in the U.S. alone. That price places the Mercedes-Benz SUV just above the fastest-growing portion of the sport-utility market. The result is that for just a few extra dollars per month a buyer can move up from a Jeep Grand Cherokee or Ford Explorer to an M-Class, thus bringing new owners into the Mercedes fold. With some 25 percent of current U.S. Mercedes-Benz owners already possessing a sport-utility vehicle, there was a built-in market for the M-Class. A higher-priced ($55,000–60,000) version of the G-Wagen likely would have had great ap-

F

peal to traditional Mercedes buyers. But this new orientation of Mercedes' SUV says a great deal about the sorts of markets and customers the company wants to include in its future plans.

There were other considerations. With perhaps as many as 40,000 M-Class vehicles for sale in America and an equivalent number available for the rest of the world, the total justified the new factory in the U.S. That factory would do double duty as a laboratory, a "learning field" for new engineering, manufacturing, business and marketing processes that could be used throughout the world.

There were also fundamental requirements. Despite the price segment, this M-Class would have to be a true Mercedes-Benz, which meant it had to include all the traditional Mercedes qualities and virtues. Early on in the program it was decided to include mechanical and technical features that would set the M-Class apart and set new standards in the sport-utility market segment.

To take advantage of the SUV knowledge already available in the company, Mercedes tapped men from the G-Wagen team to lay down the principles of the M-

Class and develop it through to production. The team was set up in a small compound outside the borders of the famous Untertürkheim factory grounds. In an inconspicuous set of buildings behind a well-guarded gate and right next to a set of railroad tracks, the development team immersed itself in this new project.

Time was tight. Learning to shrink new product development periods was just one small part of the M-Class's "learning field." Meetings were intense, often suspended momentarily on warm summer days while the noisy trains rushed by. The roads from that compound to Stuttgart's airport became an all too familiar route for those assigned to the M-Class project. There were many journeys to the hottest, coldest, highest and most humid places in the world to test this all-new vehicle in climatic extremes. And as the project moved on, more and more of those flights were aimed at the U.S., specifically to Atlanta, Georgia, with a connection to Birmingham, Alabama. A 45-minute drive west of the airport, just shy of Tuscaloosa, Alabama, the other half of the M-Class story was beginning to develop.

F **Mercedes-Benz all-wheel-drive technology is certainly no stranger to its more low-slung passenger vehicles. Case in point: this 4Matic E-Class station wagon with motorcycles in tow.**

WHERE IN THE WORLD?

Deciding to build a 4-wheel-drive sport-utility vehicle in the U.S. settled one issue for Mercedes, but created several questions. Such as where to build this new "learning field" factory. To some onlookers the choice seemed obvious, but doing the obvious was not a part of the new Mercedes-Benz plan.

In the end, it all became a stealth operation, with top-secret helicopter rides and assumed names. No photographs please.

Is this maybe a bit too dramatic?

Not when there are hundreds of millions of dollars involved. Not when thousands of jobs that will pay for rents, groceries, clothes and education are on the line. Nor is it overly dramatic for a community that can proudly say it won the new Mercedes-Benz factory, which is a most sought-after industrial prize.

That's what was at stake as Mercedes began the search for a place to situate its first U.S. factory. Although it had considered Germany and other countries, in the end it made the most sense that its sport-utility vehicle be made in the U.S., because it is the heart of the world's market for such vehicles.

Official announcement of the American factory was made on April 5, 1993. Professor Werner Niefer, then chairman and CEO of Mercedes-Benz AG, led the press conference, committing to an investment of $300 million and an employment at the factory of up to 1500 people. Helmut Werner, who succeeded the retiring Niefer the following month, made Mercedes' intentions clear when he said, "We will not withdraw into the ivory tower of building a 'mega-luxury class' sport-utility vehicle. Rather, we will attack the Japanese competition in its market niches by offering our own technologically superior products."

But where would Mercedes choose to

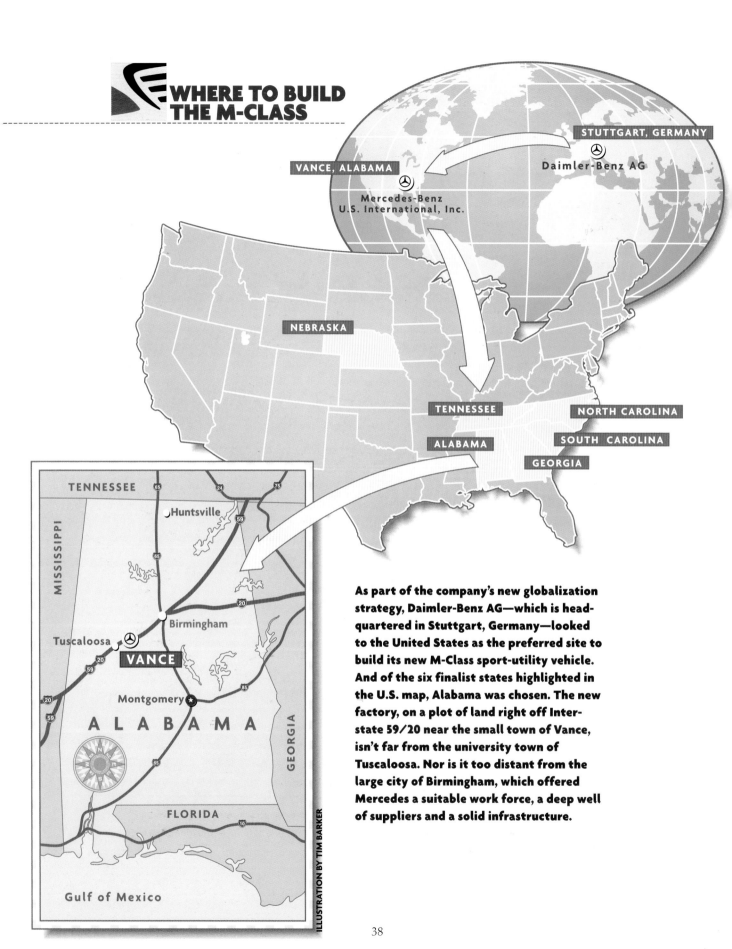

WHERE TO BUILD THE M-CLASS

STUTTGART, GERMANY

Daimler-Benz AG

VANCE, ALABAMA

Mercedes-Benz
U.S. International, Inc.

NEBRASKA

TENNESSEE

NORTH CAROLINA

ALABAMA

SOUTH CAROLINA

GEORGIA

TENNESSEE

Huntsville

MISSISSIPPI

Birmingham

Tuscaloosa

VANCE

Montgomery

A L A B A M A

GEORGIA

FLORIDA

Gulf of Mexico

ILLUSTRATION BY TIM BARKER

As part of the company's new globalization strategy, Daimler-Benz AG—which is head-quartered in Stuttgart, Germany—looked to the United States as the preferred site to build its new M-Class sport-utility vehicle. And of the six finalist states highlighted in the U.S. map, Alabama was chosen. The new factory, on a plot of land right off Inter-state 59/20 near the small town of Vance, isn't far from the university town of Tuscaloosa. Nor is it too distant from the large city of Birmingham, which offered Mercedes a suitable work force, a deep well of suppliers and a solid infrastructure.

build its factory? After the announcement, a whopping 30 of the 48 contiguous states expressed interest in the new factory. And so began another difficult phase in the M-Class story.

Site selection had started April 1, and was the responsibility of a team headed by Andreas Renschler, president of the new company known as Mercedes-Benz U.S. International, Inc. (MBUSI). The team was aided by a division of Fluor Daniel, the famous engineering firm that would build the factory. Familiar with state and community development programs around the country, Fluor Daniel's initial job was to anonymously make contacts with state and community development boards, letting them know that a multinational corporation was looking to build a manufacturing facility. The list of states was soon pared down from 30 to 21 to 12 and finally to six, which was when Mercedes' own team began visiting potential factory sites.

Stephen Cannon, a young West Point graduate and ex-army officer and the only American on the team during those early M-Class project development days in Germany, was a part of the site committee. Explains Cannon: "It was a whirlwind, but it was an interesting process. We nailed down the criteria we needed and what was important. Based on that, we created a fairly detailed decision matrix and boiled it down to six finalist states."

What was Mercedes-Benz looking for? Naturally, it wanted an area with a positive business climate, perhaps one that even had a university. Equally important, this region must have a strong and suitable work force, plus a solid infrastructure that would provide rail lines and roads to feed a new production system that would require even faster and more reliable shipment of parts into the factory than was common in the past. There also had to be proximity to a supplier base to support this different production process. And, of course, it was important to have easy shipment out to domestic dealers and to seaports from which the vehicles could be shipped abroad.

Linda Paulmeno had been plucked from her spot in the public relations department of Mercedes-Benz of North America, Inc.

A Andreas Renschler, President & CEO of Mercedes-Benz U.S. International, Inc., responsible for M-Class unit. **B** Jürgen Hubbert (left), member of the management board of Daimler-Benz AG and head of the Mercedes-Benz passenger-car division, enjoys a tour of the M-Class's Alabama factory.

to be the spokesperson for the sport-utility program. Her first office, in Chicago because of its central location, was in some space that Freightliner, a subsidiary of Mercedes-Benz, wasn't using. The office was so empty, one of her first thoughts was, "I guess I need to order pencils." Very quickly, though, Paulmeno joined the site committee—Renschler, Cannon, engineer Herb Gzik and the representative from Fluor Daniel. And her role was to make the announcement that would eventually pump hundreds of millions of dollars into a chosen community.

This is when things got rather stealthy. "We had to do this incognito," Paulmeno says, "so they'd book hotel rooms under false names and possibly have a helicopter ready to fly us to the site. We spent two nights in every location. One night the host city could entertain us, but the other night we wanted to be left alone. We wanted to see the community on our own." In addition to the government officials, the Mercedes committee talked with local business and civic leaders about such considerations as the work force and productivity.

The final six states were Tennessee, Georgia, Alabama, North Carolina, South Carolina and the sole midwest finalist, Nebraska. Although impressed by Nebraska, the higher transportation costs to and from that part of the country knocked it off the list. Eventually the site committee trimmed the list down to three

southern states: North Carolina, South Carolina and Alabama.

The fact that Alabama remained in the competition this long came as a surprise to several of those on the committee. Cannon admits he kept wondering, "When is Alabama going to fall off the list?" Renschler didn't even plan to meet the site-selection group in Alabama on their first swing through the South, but did join up at their second stop, Atlanta, Georgia. When they met in Atlanta, the group convinced Renschler he had to meet them back in Alabama because it had so much to offer.

Many of those watching from the outside dismissed Alabama. North Carolina made sense for Mercedes because the state already has factories that build its Freightliner trucks. But did it make sense to start a whole new way of building a vehicle by linking up with a part of the existing Mercedes system?

South Carolina was also expected to win, mainly because of BMW and the suppliers it had attracted to stock its Spartanburg plant. And although the state proposed a site near Charleston, that would have meant coming in as the "other German automaker."

Helping make both the Carolinas attractive were their highly-trained economic development committees, which did an excellent job of pitching their states' qualities. What Mercedes found in Alabama wasn't quite as well honed, but it was, as Cannon explains, "a real state and community pitch. It wasn't just the politicians and the state economic developers, it was also the business community that joined in and said, 'This is something we need.'"

What Alabama had to offer was the passion and determination to get the project, plus a plot of land just east of Tuscaloosa

(40 minutes west of Birmingham on Interstate 59/20) adjacent to the small town of Vance, population 250.

Still, the final selection had to be put to a vote. That happened in Germany, in the small group of buildings away from Mercedes' Untertürkheim headquarters that had become the base for the 4-wheel-drive SUV project. Now a committee of 12, including facility engineers, took a vote from two standpoints: qualitative and quantitative. Alabama won on both counts by a wide majority.

"What really sold us on Alabama,"

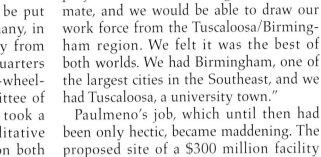

Paulmeno says, "was the commitment of the people. They were hungry for this project. There is a strong business climate, and we would be able to draw our work force from the Tuscaloosa/Birmingham region. We felt it was the best of both worlds. We had Birmingham, one of the largest cities in the Southeast, and we had Tuscaloosa, a university town."

Paulmeno's job, which until then had been only hectic, became maddening. The proposed site of a $300 million facility was understandably big news, and her phone rang day and night, at work and at home, with reporters speculating over the chosen area. Trying to keep the answer a secret as long as possible, Mercedes scheduled a press conference for Thursday, September 30, 1993. On Monday they sent out 350 invitations to the media, but instead of having the out-of-town press fly into Alabama, thereby spilling the beans, they asked them to fly to Detroit. Mercedes then chartered a 737 to ferry everyone to Alabama, keeping the site location confidential until the last minute.

Why go to all that trouble? "To have had the press conference in a neutral location would have lost the emotion," Paulmeno points out. "We wanted to have the community involved, and they were. Local people still remember that day as an historical moment. The Chamber of Commerce had it on a satellite hookup and people watched it on television in their offices, while all the kids saw it in their schools."

Called the Project Rosewood agreement, this plan could have had a thorny

C Former Alabama governor James Folsom (center) is flanked by Dr. Dieter Zetsche (right) and Renschler at the factory's groundbreaking ceremony. **D** Governor Fob James with Renschler. **E** The governor looks toward the apex, piloting an M-Class around the factory's test track.

problem when—18 months after it was signed—Fob James replaced James Folsom as governor of Alabama. Although the previous administration had made the deal with Mercedes, James declared himself fully behind the project.

And that's the sort of commitment Mercedes-Benz found for their new project in Alabama, a state that had been losing a lot of attention to such neighbors as Tennessee with GM's highly publicized Saturn factory or Georgia, which hosted the Olympic Games. Alabama needed a little shot of pride, and earned it with Mercedes-Benz.

Another automotive name, De Soto, is part of Alabama's early history. In this case it was the explorer, Hernando De Soto, who crossed the land in 1540 and used the Choctaw Indian word Alabama (meaning "to clear vegetation") for one of the rivers. Both the French and the English laid claim to the land, but the latter surrendered most of it to the United States in 1783, and in 1819 Alabama became the young country's 22nd state.

Alabama's slogan is "Heart of Dixie," and it is known historically for being the birthplace of the Confederacy. In 1861 Jefferson Davis was inaugurated president of the rebel Confederate States in the city of Montgomery. And this very same city is just as well known for being the site of possibly the most important first move in the modern civil rights movement when the Reverend Martin Luther King, Jr. directed the nonviolent bus boycotts there in 1955-56, an act prompted by the actions of another famous Alabama native, Rosa Parks. Other well-known Alabamans include singer Nat King Cole, "To Kill a Mockingbird" author Harper Lee and George Wallace, the former governor and nemesis of the Rev. King.

Although cotton was king for decades in that part of the South, manufacturing has gradually replaced it, with Birmingham being a major iron and steel center. Huntsville is well known for its ties to the aerospace industry, and Mobile offers a major seaport.

And then there's Tuscaloosa. Any American with even a little knowledge of football knows the city as the home of the University of Alabama, which is one of the perennial football powers in the country. In fact you can hardly say Alabama without the names Crimson Tide and Paul "Bear" Bryant coming out. It's a well-earned reputation, though the schools of engineering, law and liberal arts also deserve high billing. This is just one of three campuses of the university, with the others found in Birmingham and Huntsville. The university should also get credit for helping draw Mercedes-Benz to the community.

Paulmeno says the university is important to Mercedes. "It helps make this a culturally richer, more diverse community and that means better quality of life for our families. The university provides more of a melting pot in terms of culture and community, which is important for our families. The university has also established a German school for us at their cost. Teachers from Germany come here, and it's a supplemental school for the children of our German families so that when they return in three years they don't lose the German curriculum. So we've been able to tap into expertise from their management, engineering and environmental schools to help us with long-term projects."

But it's a two-way street and Mercedes has made a strong commitment to give back to the community beyond just the factory. Included in the direct outreach programs are funds to rebuild burned churches, support the Team Alabama youth soccer program and also to provide major philanthropic support for community programs in Birmingham,

F "Team Alabama," the Mercedes-Benz-sponsored youth soccer team. **G** Team Alabama in action at the Daimler-Benz Junior Cup in Stuttgart. **H** No discussion of sports in Alabama is complete without mention of the University of Alabama's "Crimson Tide" football team.

Tuscaloosa and Vance. There's also the now-annual *Weindorf,* a transplanted celebration in Tuscaloosa County of the wine harvest in Mercedes' home city of Stuttgart, Germany.

One Tuscaloosa resident, Jack Leigh, has benefited directly from the Mercedes-Benz factory. His family has been the local Mercedes-Benz dealer for 16 years. Sitting behind the desk in his dealership, Leigh says, "For years I had so many people who would come up to me and say, 'Jack, I'd love to have a Mercedes and one of these days I'm going to have one, but right now I can't let my patients or my clients or my employees see me in one.' Now they say, 'I'm being patriotic by buying a Mercedes. Here these people are investing so much in Tuscaloosa County and I need to support them.' So it gave them an excuse to come and buy, and we've sold cars to people who never would have bought one in the past."

As someone who grew up in Tusca-

loosa County, Leigh also has a broader view, explaining that, "If one of the coal mining companies had decided to expand with 1500 employees or open a new mine it would have been a one-day story in the paper. Mercedes scouring the whole country, even looking all over the world, then deciding on Alabama allowed us to get rid of a lot of baggage we've been carrying for years about being the old South with the dogs under the porch and that sort of thing. Mercedes put us more in the new South, with Georgia, the Carolinas and Tennessee."

Leigh also speaks of the physical changes that have come to Tuscaloosa County. "You can see German programs on the cable channel. If you'd been through the downtown area several years ago, many buildings were boarded up. Now we're getting new restaurants and we've quietly become an international city. It started a while back when the Japanese came with JVC, Michelin bought the tire plant which was originally a BFGoodrich factory, and the British are here with Tuscaloosa Steel, a subsidiary of British Steel. So when Mercedes came, I think of a lot of investors who thought we might be short term realized we aren't. You can't drive out of Tuscaloosa without seeing property leveled and building going on...and those people buy cars." And Jack Leigh is building a new dealership.

█With German employees comes German culture, embodied by music, dress and song at this wine harvest celebration. █Friendly Mercedes billboards announce the new M-Class factory.

Charles Nash, Vice Chancellor for academic affairs for the University of Alabama Systems, talks about the effects of the Mercedes project on the community as having "given us an opportunity to think about horizons that we probably hadn't dreamed were out there, making it possible to imagine other avenues of opportunity that are out there."

Speaking as a member of the African-American community he adds, "The African-American community, generally speaking, has a high level of diversity and I think it sees the German influence as a positive continuation of caring about and raising diversity."

He points out that Tuscaloosa County is in pretty good economic shape, but says that nearby areas are suffering. While the Mercedes factory will eventually provide 1500 jobs, its influence goes deeper and creates other jobs.

"I think it says to black adults, as well as black youth, that there are job opportunities. Yes, you have to prepare yourself. Yes, it's going to be competitive, but, yes, there are also opportunities to improve yourself. I think it gives us all some hope, particularly the African-American community, that our kids can grow up here, go to school in the area and come back and work here and not have to go off to New York or Chicago or Florida to find a good job."

What sort of styling should Mercedes-Benz's new sport-utility vehicle have? American? German? Japanese? And how will this new vehicle's design enable it to fit into the Mercedes product lineup? For that matter, what makes a Mercedes look like a Mercedes? Those were among the many questions answered by designers around the world.

SKETCHES, CLAY & METAL

June, 1993, and the viewing arena in Mercedes-Benz's Sindelfingen design center looked a bit like a sport-utility sales lot...though a very exotic one. All the vehicles in the exhibit wore the Mercedes star and had never been seen in public. In progress was a top secret viewing of what the company's proposed All-Activity Vehicle (M-Class) might look like, and on display were one U.S., one Japanese and three German variations on a fundamental American theme.

The theme originated with American

pickup trucks. They were the basis for the U.S. and, later, the Japanese contenders in the fast-growing SUV market. And for better or worse they looked like their roots. It made financial, marketing and engineering sense for the vehicles built off a truck basis to share fundamental form and, often, sheet metal with the pickups. Originally several of the entries even looked like pickup trucks with camper shells, though as the market has matured sport-utility machines have taken on more character of their own. There

start the M-Class styling process without any of these pickup encumbrances. And they were even looking to break away from the one in-house vehicle with which their new sport utility would share some heritage, the Geländewagen.

In fact, one of the full-size clay models in the Sindelfingen studio was a proposed redo of the squarish Mercedes G-Wagen, which made its debut in early 1979 and was originally designed more with military use and sales in mind than with any thought of being a serious contender in the expanding upscale sport-utility market. A handsome machine, this updated G-Wagen showed only the wheels of the older model and a hint of heritage in the grille area before blending back into a dramatically smoother, obviously "civilianized" machine.

While this new Geländewagen might have been able to compete against the likes of the Range Rover and the Toyota Land Cruiser in the $50,000-and-up market segment, it didn't fit into Mercedes' new market-driven strategy. This new price-conscious thinking called for a sport utility with a different character than the G-Wagen, one that aimed at a new point on the demographic map and that could be popularly priced in the mid-$30,000 range to take on the better-equipped Ford Explorers and Jeep Grand Cherokees.

Design sketches were already being made in late 1992, even though the decision had not yet been made about the wheelbase (or wheelbases) of the new M-Class. Early drawings depicted 4-door models and several rather dramatic 2-door, short-wheelbase possibilities to appeal to sportier drivers.

remains, however, a definite tie to their origins, which has some esthetic drawbacks, perhaps, but also lends an air of sporty utility and ruggedness.

Mercedes-Benz designers were able to

A Designers in Mercedes' California studio review early sketches. **B** California crew with a side elevation of a 2-door M-Class concept. **C** Peter Arcadipane works on a 2-door proposal in Germany.

D

The styling of the M-Class was a process that involved three major design proposals from Mercedes' studios in Sindelfingen and one each from the company's advanced design facilities in California and Japan.

Mercedes-Benz's Chief of Design, Bruno Sacco, summarizes the basic aim of the project when he points out that, "What we did not want to do was develop just another SUV, a me-too product, the umpteenth version of existing SUVs. So

D Designers try detail changes to an early scale model in Mercedes-Benz's Sindelfingen studio.

we determined what this SUV should look like, what it should have in both on- and off-road characteristics. The styling of the vehicle was to convey that you could use it on the highways and city streets, of course, but not only there because many people would use it for both on-road and off-road operation and we wanted to include that possibility in our design concept."

Getting that balance of on- and off-road appearance, of elegance and sportiness, proved an interesting challenge for the designers. The Japanese studio, which had only just been formed, was doing its potential M-Class as its first major project.

The clay model of Mercedes' Advanced Design studio in Irvine, California, reflected that state's unique lifestyle and long involvement with off-roading. It was originally done as a 2-door model that could be built on the same wheelbase-length chassis. Being aware of the company's emphasis on attracting younger buyers, the designers in Irvine didn't want the 2-door completely neglected. Their model featured a removable rear "bubble" shell that could be lifted off to create a sort of semi-convertible. In order to be comparable in the final decision with all the other 4-door models, the Irvine studio was asked to present a 4-door version on the passenger side of their model as well. Interestingly, a huge mirror in the rear allowed evaluation of both versions pseudo-symmetrically from each three-quarter angle. The 2-door was put on hold because marketing studies showed only a marginal interest in it.

Having a muscular shape with fender flares, and a tall, strong front end that nicely integrates the Mercedes grille, the U.S. model was thought to be aimed a bit too much at a younger, off-road oriented audience than was intended for the M-Class.

This design would later resurface as the All-Activity Vehicle show car.

The three Sindelfingen entries varied greatly. One used a greenhouse window treatment that made it look too much like a minivan. A second shape had a front end that mirrored some of the thinking in the updated G-Wagen, plus a distinctive rear-sloping C-pillar that brought with it a direct design link to the company's new A-Class city car. The third design, however, was the only one that featured just the right balance of Mercedes elegance and off-road capability. This model was developed into the production M-Class.

What made this model the final choice reflects what Mercedes Design considers its approach to the sport-utility market. Dieter Futschik, who heads the design group that styled the M-Class explains, "What we tried to do was bring together different sorts of characters. First of all was the Mercedes appeal. We tried to do a very elegant form with the formal language of a real passenger vehicle. While there was not to be so much of an off-road vehicle in the shape, we tried to bring to the concept car some elements that could remind one of an off-road vehicle. So we had a little balance of these two characters."

One of the most impressive things about Mercedes-Benz passenger vehicles is that they are instantly recognizable as a member of the Mercedes family, and that ability to be recognized cuts across geographic and language barriers around the world. Making this facet a cornerstone of the design of the ground-breaking M-Class was crucial, and logically makes one ask: What is it that makes a Mercedes a Mercedes?

Says Bruno Sacco: "It's no easy task to ensure that we have a family tie between a small Mercedes car or SUV and a rela-

tively large Mercedes, which are used for rather different applications. So what we do have is a bracket that consists of various design and marque elements which have been developed and consolidated over the course of time.

"The Mercedes grille, the SL grille, is a good example. Through sophisticated modifications and adjustments we have made these into design elements that ensure these vehicles belong to one family. And, of course, we make use of other elements that are used time and again and that make it easier for an observer to see

E Earliest design proposal was for an updated, softer version of the G-Wagen. **F** One intended M-Class design shared the unique upswept C-pillar of Mercedes' A-Class. **G** German clay modelers prepare a full-scale M-Class. **H** Dramatic front of an M-Class from the California studio.

that it is a Mercedes-Benz car. The fender to A-pillar transition, wheelwells, the sides of the vehicle, the shape of the lamps...this bracket has been developed for the different cars and contains the common elements."

Futschik adds that creating a Mercedes

goes well beyond the matter of where to put the famous star. "I think the character of the car comes from a team that is working very long on the same themes. It can't be as easily described as saying, 'Well, this is a Mercedes turn signal and here is where the star must go.' That's not what

I Perhaps the most carlike, this proposal's nose has strong ties to Mercedes sedans... **J** ...and a very adventurous, rather odd rear glass treatment. **K** California's proposal was parked next to a Jeep for comparison. **L** Both 2- and 4-door models were built on the same wheelbase.

INTERIEUR 2

INTERIEUR 4

makes a Mercedes a Mercedes. The real character comes in the way all this is produced by our team. Our designers have their typical style, and when this continues over a long time, throughout an entire model line, you can create a similar character among all those automobiles.

"How you shape the lines and the planes, how that plays together, the harmony between these planes, how the detailing is done, how all that is thought through…all these things become typical of the Mercedes appearance…just as other coachbuilders have their own style. And you can't easily say this is why you do this or do that…it's just their style. You can recognize a Bertone car very easily because he has his own way of designing cars…and so do we.

"We have a very good team, very creative people and the way we work is that we are not separated into different studios as some companies are, but our designers are working on every project so in the end there is a similarity among all models. And that's how you give a Mercedes character to a new vehicle."

All of this had to be adapted to this newest of Mercedes, one that would have to wear, the Mercedes-Benz design themes on new and taller proportions. Starting with that famous "face."

Since the Fifties there has been a distinction made with Mercedes-Benz

M Suggested interior designs included one from California. **N** An alternative from Sindelfingen.
O And the approved interior, which was developed into… **P** …the production layout.
Q Franz-Josef Siegert, here sketching a proposal, is credited with design of the M-Class interior.

R S To hint at the upcoming M-Class, Mercedes-Benz had its California Advanced Design Studio create the All-Activity Vehicle, which was an auto show star in 1996. **T** Design team included, from left, André Frey, Richard Plavetich, Michael Ma, Melonee Ranziger, Gerhard Steinle, Benjamin Dimson and Paul Terry.

grilles. Today's Mercedes sedans have the classic, formal upright face that can draw a philosophical line back through the renowned SSKs of the Thirties to the trio of Mercedes that finished 1-2-3 in their historical win in the 1914 French Grand Prix. Modern sporting Mercedes carry a more horizontal grille that traces its beginning to the famous 300SL in the Fifties. And so the tradition continues today. As the M-Class is a passenger vehicle

with sporting possibilities, it takes on a horizontal grille that, as Bruno Sacco explains, "…has been adjusted and is now more sporty, a kind of philosophical crossbreed between the SL radiator mask and the typical Mercedes face."

Headlamps for the M-Class also draw from Mercedes' sporting side, reminiscent of the S-Class coupe and the SLK, and yet with a unique look. Sacco points out another Mercedes feature in the way the

Design of the production M-Class marries the sport-utility image with Mercedes-Benz style.

58

front fender runs into the A-pillar. "This transition is highly typical and similar to the front fender running into the A-pillar of the SL convertible from 1989, and it is a design feature you also see on the C-Class and A-Class."

At one point, designers considered eliminating the C-pillar and creating a unique glass greenhouse, but this made the M-Class look too much like a crossbred SUV/minivan and was abandoned. The wider C-pillar in the final design is one of those elements meant to hint at the off-road potential of the M-Class. The back of the vehicle has no tie to Mercedes heritage because there has never been a vehicle quite like the M-Class in the company's lineup. And yet you know it's a Mercedes even from behind because the taillight shape draws heavily on that used in the SLK...again an example of the same people and the same theme creating elements that are not identical, but similar in their characteristics. Another Mercedes design cue is the roof rails, which were adopted from the company's station wagons.

Like most modern vehicles, the M-Class did its time in the wind tunnel, and the aim was to make it the most aerodynamically efficient sport-utility vehicle on the market. This is a most difficult task because the basic size and square shape of SUVs mean they have coefficient of drag numbers well above those of many automobiles. Mercedes aerodynamicists maintained that there wasn't much progress to be made with that sort of blocky front end—though a small lower spoiler was added—but they could have an effect by revising the slope of the roof from the front to the back of the M-Class, which they did, squaring it off a bit. Wind tunnel work was also done on the outside rearview mirrors to minimize noise and,

because safety is a cornerstone of every Mercedes, to keep the mirror surface and the side windows as clean as possible in foul weather. Despite its shape, the M-Class has a drag coefficient of 0.39, meaning it's more slippery than its competitors, such as the Jeep Grand Cherokee at 0.45.

Mercedes designers weren't just working on a new type of vehicle, they were also dealing with several new processes. One was simultaneous engineering, which meant the designers and the engineers creating the mechanical parts of the M-Class started working together earlier, more closely, and in smaller groups, than with past projects.

Relying on suppliers to provide major subsystems for the M-Class "just in time" to the factory in Alabama also involved the designers working with representatives of various other companies from early on in the design stage.

This relationship with outside companies was possibly the closest inside the M-Class, where there are a number of complicated subsystems—such as the seats and the dashboard—that are preassembled and delivered to the factory. As an example of the new automaker-supplier ties, the last thing the Mercedes design department did with the seats was to provide a final mockup in which all the surfaces were described mathematically. The seat maker took development from there, only involving Mercedes when there were minor changes needed for technical or manufacturing reasons.

Those seats, the dashboard and all the elements of the interior were also decided upon after studying the designs from the German, American and Japanese studios. Futschik explains that, "What we saw from the competitive vehicles already on the market were interiors that reminded us very much of commercial vehicles… very edgy, very square. We tried to make it a bit different, with more rounded forms, more passenger-carlike forms in a way that was very practical so you can say that you are sitting in a car where you can feel good…the exception to that car sensation being that we think it's a very good feeling to sit a little bit higher above the traffic as you do in an SUV. Women, in particular, appreciate that and they are extremely important in the SUV market place." In fact, in the initial phase women were asked what they would like in an SUV. Their comments about low step-in height, easy access to the rear cargo area and lots of storage space affected the final design.

Again it was the design from Sindelfingen that got the nod. And again you can see that the result comes from a team that is following a well established line of thinking. Marketing asked for seating for five or more adults in the M-Class and the result is a seat package and appearance that immediately remind one of the interior of Mercedes-Benz station wagons. The steering wheel, instrument panel graphics, vents, door handles and the tasteful use of wood paneling will tell anyone who has driven a Mercedes that the M-Class is part of the family.

Bruno Sacco comments that doing the interior for the M-Class was a bit more difficult than designing an interior for one of Mercedes' automobiles. He begins by admitting that, "Actually it was quite fun to design the interior of the M-Class, and the designers had quite a large influence on the packaging." Adds Sacco: "What plays a major role in an SUV is the variability of the interior. With classi-cal designs you have a correlation between the interior and exterior design and the two can influence each other. Then you can create common features. It is more difficult with a functionally-oriented car like the M-Class—especially when it is functionally oriented inside—because the exterior design does not really influence the interior design. And yet despite this functional approach, you also have to consider that people have to find it comfortable and convenient to ride in the car, and that it gives them pleasure, so you also have to add the correct esthetic and comfort elements."

In the end, mixing function, comfort and off-road with elegance produced an M-Class design that Dieter Futschik terms international style with a Continental twist. "It is a little bit European, when you look at the materials, the way it is done, how it is oriented…I think American style would have been more enlarged. I think that's a difference. What we wanted to do was avoid American style because I think the customers expect that a Mercedes-Benz is not American. They want to have the European origin and I think it would disturb them a little bit if you would say, 'Okay this is made by Mercedes but it looks very American.'"

Americans did get a brief look at a more American approach to the M-Class. With the development of the M-Class on fast forward and the factory getting closer to completion, Mercedes-Benz U.S. International, Inc. figured it was time to give the public a small hint of what its new baby would look like. Target date was January 3, 1996, and the Mercedes-Benz press conference at the North American International Auto Show in Detroit. Several

▼ **The production M-Class, both rugged and dignified in appearance.**

developing Mercedes designs, particularly the E-Class round-headlamp front end and the SLK sports car, had been shown to the public in advance in surprisingly undisguised form.

Gerhard Steinle, who heads the California studio, put his designers to work modifying the design because, "We knew that it would be a show car, so we exaggerated some areas, like the fender flares, wheels and things like that." Given the freedom to do what they liked like in the interior, Steinle's studio created a fresh interpretation of Mercedes' style.

The results? Rave reports by the motoring press and *AutoWeek* magazine's award as "Best of Show."

When the All-Activity Vehicle was unveiled at Detroit, the final design of the M-Class had been "frozen" for some 21 months. Orders for tooling and the thousands of pieces that make up the vehicle required that much lead time to begin arriving at Tuscaloosa for just-in-time production. Still, the designers' job didn't really end with the design freeze. There might not have been as many women and men working on the car, but any production vehicle becomes something of a perpetual project. There had to be modifications developed for the V-8 model, which would be along within the first year. Model changes and updates are an unavoidable reality of today's auto market, and they require lead time also. What mattered most, however, was that the M-Class style had been established, and it slotted nicely and appropriately into the Mercedes-Benz family.

LIVING PROOF

Safety and quality are two cornerstones of Mercedes-Benz's engineering philosophy, and integral parts of every passenger car it sells. As engineers began their work on the M-Class sport-utility vehicle, they were determined to ensure that their new SUV had these same traits— from top to bottom.

It's an automotive engineer's dream. Mercedes-Benz, which is famous for its strong engineering foundation, assigns you to design a new vehicle, a type never before made by the company. You get to start with a clean sheet of paper and put the essence of Mercedes' proud tradition of safety, quality, roadholding and performance into this new machine. For good measure, the company throws in a new manufacturing system in a different country. And there's a revised way of dealing with suppliers and the various departments within Mercedes itself.

This sounds like a dream that could cost an engineer a lot of sleep.

That dream became reality in early 1993 when Mercedes' board of management approved the plan to build this new vehicle. Although product planners looked at both minivans and a model that might bridge the gap between a minivan and a sport-utility vehicle, it quickly became obvious that an SUV was the proper direction. In the past, Mercedes would have then begun design and development of the new product, but the new Mercedes-Benz prefers to listen first to the voice of the customer. Clinics were held in the U.S. and Europe to quiz SUV owners about the good and bad points of their vehicles so that Mercedes could better develop an M-Class that would satisfy market demands.

As those answers were fed into the system to define the M-Class, they became part of a new process Mercedes was trying with its "learning field" sport-utility project. Marketing manager Stephen Cannon, who has been with the group almost from the beginning, explains, "The old development process was like a relay race. The first guys to get the baton were the designers and developers. They'd run around the track, do their job, and then hand off the baton to the manufacturing guys, who would figure out tooling and how to put the manufacturing process into place. Next the baton would go to the cost guys, who would turn the crank and say, 'This is what it's going to cost.' And then, finally, marketing got the baton.

"For the M-Class, we created function groups. The vehicle was broken down into components—the cockpit, the drivetrain,

the chassis assembly—which were logical segments. These groups were then manned with cost controllers, development engineers, a marketing guy, somebody from manufacturing, another from service and supply, so they could all interact from the beginning of the project.

"Each of those function groups had cost targets, time targets and weight targets. They were empowered within those targets to make the decisions, thus cutting time from the project."

Fairly early in the process other members were added to each group, and they were outsiders...another unusual move for Mercedes-Benz. Dr. Gerhard Fritz, who headed the M-Class development team, says that in the simultaneous engineering that took place within the function groups, "Designers talked with engineers who talked with cost accountants and so forth, and an important addition was also talking with our suppliers."

A **Scenes from some automotive boneyard? Not exactly. The facility is Mercedes' German skunkworks; the parts are from M-Class prototypes that have cumulatively accrued hundreds of thousands of test miles in the quest for the reliability that has made Mercedes famous.**

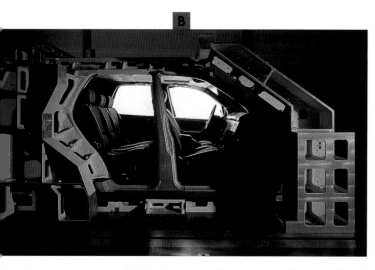

Including suppliers was the result of another inventive aspect of the M-Class plan, which called for the vehicle to be assembled from large subsystems—a completed dashboard, finished seats, etc.—rather than with thousands of smaller parts. Those major components would be provided by suppliers who had been given the responsibility for their subsystems' final design work. As a result, these "outsiders" had to be members of the teams from the beginning, rather than being handed a set of plans late in the game and asked to come back with pallets of parts.

As the M-Class development continued, this new manufacturing system was an important consideration, because the M-Class had to be assembled in Alabama with all the quality a buyer expects from a Mercedes that was built in Sindelfingen or Bremen.

The function groups set up camp at a place called Weisserth & Hieber, a small engineering outpost on Augsburger Strasse, close—but not too close—to Mercedes-Benz's headquarters in Untertürkheim. Jürgen Benkwitz, who man-

aged development of the M-Class's body and trim, says the teams were made up of "different engineers coming from the passenger car department, the truck department and also from the G-Wagen department, so it was really a great opportunity to gather all this knowledge to create the M-Class."

The various function groups were charged with turning the M-Class concepts of cast iron, sheet steel, aluminum, plastic and leather into reality. With the heavy use of computers and finite element analysis, they were able to quickly lay down the basics of this SUV, which would bring Mercedes' basic values into a new market segment.

Paramount among Mercedes' values is safety, which can be divided into two areas—passive and active. Both of these have played an important role in the design and development of the M-Class.

Active safety, in simple terms, has to do with avoiding the accident in the first place. Passive safety, on the other hand, is what protects the occupants when hope is lost and the crash is inevitable. Facing this dark but occasional reality played an instrumental role in creating the M-Class's robust structure.

There are two common ways to design a vehicle. The first and more traditional method involves a sturdy metal frame to which the suspension, driveline and body are mounted. The second method, often called a unit body, features a load-carrying body made up of several stampings strong enough to carry the drivetrain and suspension without a separate frame.

Mercedes-Benz automobiles are made this way, while its famous Geländewagen

B To ensure uniformity in the M-Class's structure, this "perfect" body buck was constructed.
C A disguised prototype of the M-Class undergoing a test at the Alabama factory.

C

sport-utility vehicle has a separate frame and body. One of the first decisions by the engineering team was to choose which type of construction would be used for the M-Class.

After careful study, much of it by computer, the team settled on the body-on-frame design. There was a practical reason for this, one brought on by Mercedes' newness to the non-military SUV market: It would be easier to modify a part of the frame, if needed, than to rework a unit body.

The M-Class frame has two longitudinal box-section side rails connected by three transverse crossmembers. While it bears a resemblance to the frame under the G-Wagen, it is significantly lighter, weighing 264 lb. versus 440. This was possible because the frame under the M-Class serves a somewhat different purpose than the G-Wagen's. The older de-sign used the frame for much of its torsional (anti-twisting) stiffness. In the M-Class, though, the body provides 70 percent of the total torsional rigidity, with the frame accounting for 30 percent. The body—which is as stiff as that of an E-Class, thanks in part to its eight sturdy triple-layer roof pillars—is joined to the frame through 10 rubber mounts that help insulate the driver and passengers from road noise and vibration.

The M-Class frame is not, however, merely a place to attach the driveline and suspensions; it also plays a crucial role in passive safety. The front and rear cross-members have designed-in "crash boxes" that absorb energy by deforming in an accident. Among other things, these boxes will prevent damage to the long side rails in a minor shunt, lowering the cost of repair. In a big crash, the frame will bend in concert with the body, which has its own

designed-in crumple zones, all the better to keep crash energy out of the passenger compartment.

This commitment to safety is nothing new for Mercedes-Benz, which pioneered research into the subject as early as 1939. By 1953, Mercedes put its concept of isolating a vehicle's occupants in a rigid passenger cabin into production with its 180 model. The idea is to let the frame, front and rear sheet metal, even the spare tire, take the punishment. Driver and passengers, meantime, are surrounded by a safety cage. Mercedes also likes to point out that the M-Class, as with its automobiles, is designed not just for straight-in barrier crashes demanded by government regulations, but also for difficult offset impacts

that more closely duplicate typical real-world accidents.

The safety details of the M-Class go far beyond just the design of the frame and body. The standards for the 19.2-gallon plastic fuel tank were inherited from the G-Wagen, where military specifications were required. The tank is located in a protected area inside the robust frame rails. If an M-Class is ever rammed right at the gas cap location, the tank's filler pipe can rip free without damage to fuel tank integrity.

Sturdy, wedge-shape strikers for the door locks and strong hinges work together with the side door beams to help make up the passenger safety cage, transmitting side-impact energy to the roof pillars. And

Safety is of paramount importance in all Mercedes-Benz vehicles. To that end, the M-Class line is equipped with a full complement of airbags for both frontal and side impacts.

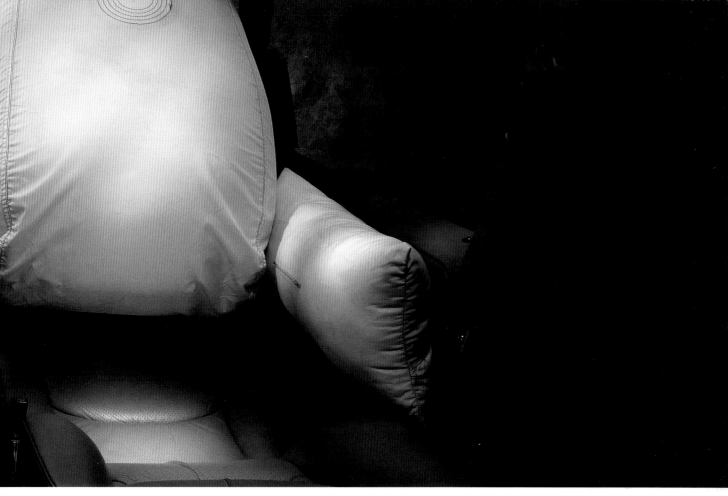

reach-through door handles on the M-Class offer the most leverage for anyone trying to open a crumpled door. Supplementing the dual frontal-impact airbags are side-impact airbags mounted in each front door. These are an M-Class exclusive among sport-utility vehicles.

Other safety enhancements include a front end design that is "pedestrian considerate," sturdy seat frames and adjustable shoulder anchors for the front and outside second row seatbelts, which have emergency tensioners and belt-force limiters.

The M-Class chassis design, however, is meant to keep the driver from having that accident in the first place. This is the active safety side of the subject, and the objective was to imbue the M-Class with the same highly respected handling characteristics as the company's sedans.

The starting point is the suspension, an

M-CLASS CHASSIS

Heart of the M-Class's 4wd system is the transfer case, mated to the 5-speed automatic transmission.

Nestled snugly between the frame rail and the rear driveshaft, the M-Class's 19.2-gal. fuel tank is well protected in the event of a crash.

The M-Class's aluminum-wishbone independent rear suspension is much lighter than a live axle setup, offering better compliance and ride comfort.

Front suspension design differs from Mercedes' passenger-car practice in that torsion bars are used for springing. The lower wishbone here is steel; all others are forged aluminum.

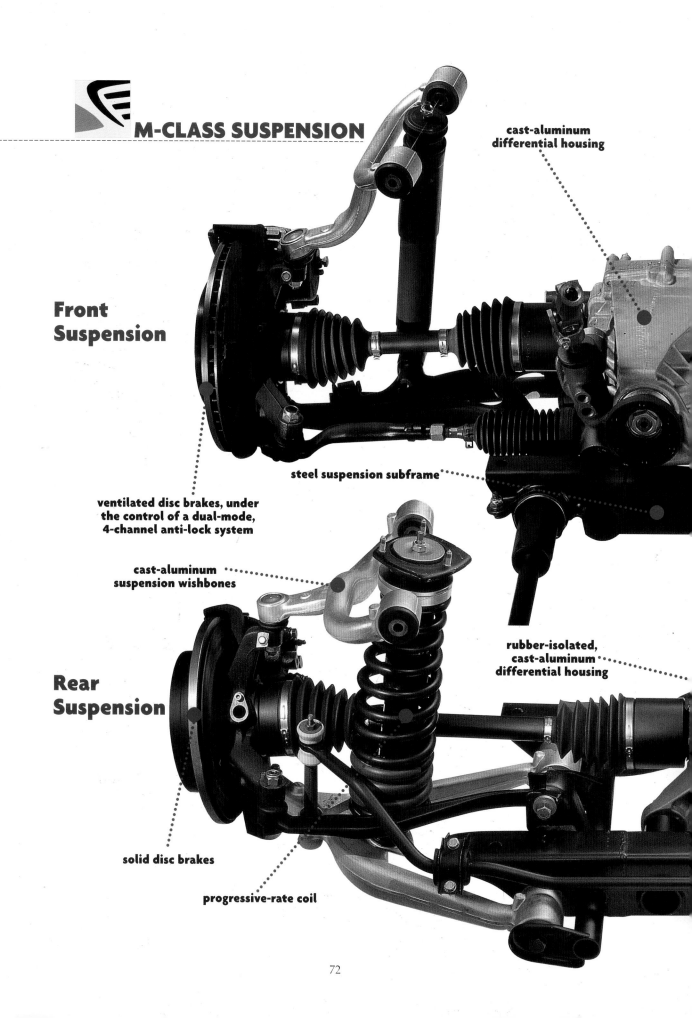

M-CLASS SUSPENSION

**cast-aluminum
differential housing**

**Front
Suspension**

steel suspension subframe

**ventilated disc brakes, under
the control of a dual-mode,
4-channel anti-lock system**

**cast-aluminum
suspension wishbones**

**rubber-isolated,
cast-aluminum
differential housing**

**Rear
Suspension**

solid disc brakes

progressive-rate coil

72

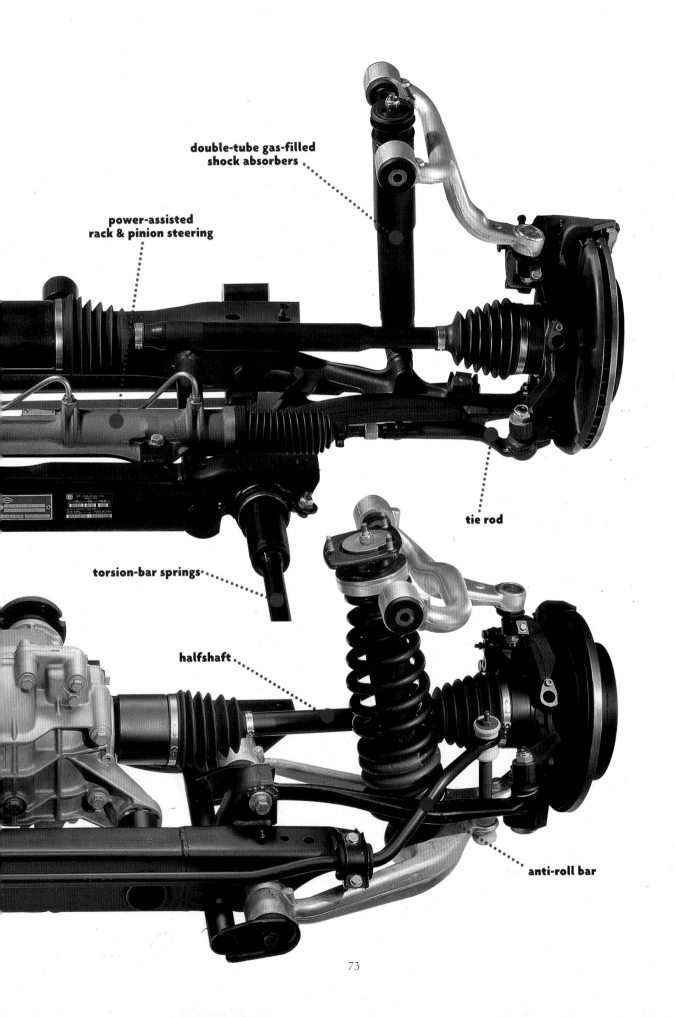

double-tube gas-filled
shock absorbers

power-assisted
rack & pinion steering

tie rod

torsion-bar springs

halfshaft

anti-roll bar

area in which having a clean sheet of paper—and not needing to adapt a truck-based design—provides a clear advantage for the M-Class.

While many current sport utilities have independent front suspension, a few still use a "live" axle. Mercedes goes the independent route, with upper and lower A-arms, the top one forged from aluminum, the lower arm being steel. For reasons of packaging and crash-energy management, the front springing is by torsion bars, which are unusual for a Mercedes automobile but have been used in the company's light trucks. Double-tube gas-filled shock absorbers are fitted to this front suspension, and an anti-roll bar connects the lower control arms.

The lower arms and the aluminum rack-and-pinion steering are carried on a subframe that bolts to the main frame and helps isolate noise and vibration. The upper suspension arms and shock absorbers are connected directly to the frame. Aluminum is used for the differential housing, which is attached to the frame at three rubber mounts, again to reduce transmission of noise and vibration to the body.

What makes the M-Class unique is that while most other SUVs use a "live" rear axle, the Mercedes rear suspension is in-dependent, quite similar to the front, including the subframe mounting. Minor differences include using both upper and lower suspension arms of aluminum, and progressive-rate coil springs replacing the torsion bars.

A major advantage for the M-Class is that its suspension is as much as 66 percent lighter than those of competitive SUVs. Matched to the very rigid body, this dramatically lower unsprung weight translates directly into better ride and handling characteristics. All-independent suspension also means the M-Class can sit lower to the ground, making it easier to get into and out of than other SUVs. Off-roaders will like the independent suspension because of its abundant wheel travel and ability to adapt to uneven surfaces.

Another important component of the M-Class is its disc brakes, which are as large as those of any other SUV. And, of course, the M-Class has ABS. Not, however, just any anti-lock, but a diagonal 4-channel system with a special program in low range for loose road surfaces.

While standard ABS works beautifully on solid, dry pavement, there are slippery lower friction surfaces where it will likely act somewhat differently. ABS, in fundamental terms, senses a locked wheel and releases its brake, and then reapplies it,

repeating this process many times per second. This action allows the vehicle to be steered while braking, and it may shorten stopping distances. On loose surfaces such as dirt roads, however, it's actually best to allow a bit of wheel lockup. When the M-Class is traveling in low range on a loose surface (which is detected by the ABS/4ETS wheel-speed sensors), the Mercedes anti-lock hardware automatically changes to a program that will stop the vehicle quicker and much more effectively.

Those disc brakes are tucked inside 255/65-16 tires on 16-in. aluminum alloy wheels, which are probably a bit larger than Mercedes' engineers would prefer. In Europe, the M-Class has 225/75-16s, but Americans like bigger tires on their SUVs. And if that's what the customers want, that's what they'll get. Interestingly, the engineers had to add extra sound insulation in the rear wheelwells, the firewall and the floor to get the noise level of the U.S. M-Class back up to Mercedes' high standards.

The steering, which is important for the part it plays in handling and active safety, also delivers an immediate impression to the driver of Mercedes' quality. Engineers adopted a system similar to the power-assisted rack and pinion used in the new Mercedes E-Class sedans. The results are a tight turning circle and the sort of response that's a fitting complement to the fine handling of the M-Class.

The steering also telegraphs to the driver that she or he is driving a Mercedes, in the same vein as the C- or E-Class sedans. Helmut Gilbert, the senior manager for chassis development, explains: "We asked our experts from the passenger car side how it is possible to get the same feeling in the M-Class as in our cars. I think it was a good idea to ask them, and I think we've achieved this."

Making certain their sport-utility vehicle had the same steering feel, the same active and passive safety capabilities, quality, roadholding and ride traits of their automobiles is just the sort of challenge the Mercedes engineers relished.

Jürgen Benkwitz, the body and trim manager of the M-Class, summed up the engineers' approach to the design and development of the vehicle when he explained, "That's the Mercedes-Benz experience. It's difficult to describe, and nearly impossible for me to specifically point out what you do to create a car like this. In the end, it comes from the experience of all the people in the engineering department…it's Mercedes-Benz and we don't know any other way to do it."

THE HEART OF THE MATTER

The development of the M-Class paralleled that of a new family of Mercedes powerplants being made in Bad Cannstatt, where Gottlieb Daimler experimented with his original single-cylinder engine.

Engines started it all. And they also separated Gottlieb Daimler and Karl Benz from the men who *almost* invented the first automobile. There was no mechanical mystery to the wheels, belts or steering gears of those early horseless carriages, but timing of the engine's spark and properly atomizing the fuel for the first internal-combustion engines befuddled many a fine inventor.

Since those first single-cylinder fire-breathers, the history of Daimler, Benz and then Mercedes-Benz has been one continuous strand of excellently designed and meticulously assembled powerplants. And there's no reason to expect anything less from M 112, the V-6 that will power the M-Class in America. Mercedes has always given its engines rather pedestrian labels—no Thunderbird V-8s or Blue Flame sixes—but this has done nothing to lessen their excellent reputations.

Daimler, Benz and Mercedes-Benz history also includes a long succession of inline engines, with 4-cylinders being used as early as 1899 and 6-cylinders since 1906. Inline-8s were used in many of the most famous sports and racing Mercedes, including the prewar 500/540Ks and Grand Prix cars, and the renowned 300SLR and W196 race cars of the mid-Fifties. As well as inline engines have served Mercedes-Benz, however, new packaging demands—such as the lower hoodlines of new smaller automobiles—made it evident Mercedes needed a shorter, more compact 6-cylinder engine. A smaller powerplant would also have crash safety advantages, making it easier to provide crush zones to aid in energy-dissipating deformation.

With rapidly evolving developments in engine technology, Mercedes was ready for a new family of engines that would include both V-6 and V-8 aluminum blocks with a vee angle of 90 degrees. The powerplants would be made on the same assembly lines in a new factory in Bad Cannstatt, near Stuttgart. To calm the inherent imbalances of the 90-degree V-6, the engine would be fitted with a counter-rotating balance shaft spinning at the same speed as the crankshaft.

Beginning with the classic clean sheet of paper, Mercedes designers were able to concentrate on making the engines not only small, but also light. The weight of the 3.2-liter V-6 has been trimmed by an impressive 25 percent compared to its straight-6 predecessor of the same displacement, for a savings of about 110 lb. Credit for the savings goes to such techniques as aluminum and magnesium pressure diecasting, a new aluminum-silicon cylinder-liner technology, a sheet-steel exhaust manifold and lightweight "cracked" steel connecting rods.

The newest advance in the V-6 is its light alloy cylinder liners, that were jointly developed by Mercedes-Benz and PEAK. Called "Silicon Liner Technology" or, "Silitec," this process coats the cylinder liner wall surface with a special aqueous treatment to reduce the friction caused by the piston rings making contact with the bore. This new technology does away with heavy cast-iron cylinder liners, saving more than a pound per cylinder. It also lessens noise, reduces cylinder deformation and allows better heat flow to the crankcase. The secret is in the way the working surface is treated, a process that Mercedes-Benz and PEAK will sell to any other automakers.

Iron-coated cast-aluminum pistons connect to the crankshaft via forged-steel rods that are 25 percent lighter than those of the inline-6. They are also more precise, thanks to a technique that allows their big ends to be cracked and rejoined, rather than machined.

One example of the lightweight diecast-

A Though sharing the same displacement (3199 cc), bore and stroke (89.9 mm x 84.0 mm) and compression ratio (10.0:1) as the company's respected inline-6, the 215-bhp M 112 V-6 is all new.

A

ing lies beneath the crankshaft: a sump that weighs only 57 lb. versus 121 for that of the inline-6. More weight saving also took place in the new diecast-aluminum cylinder heads. The number of camshafts in the cylinder heads has been reduced from two to one, and a fully machined hollow cast-iron cam also saves weight. Each cam now opens the valves by way of low-friction roller-type rocker arms instead of the tappets used in the previous engines. And they open fewer valves as this V-6 has two intake valves and a single exhaust valve per cylinder.

Why not use the popular 4-valve layout? Mercedes' tests found that by eliminating one exhaust valve there was less heat loss between the engine and the catalytic converter, which is important in lowering exhaust emissions. (This technique, incidentally, applies to the V-6. The inline-4s—which generally work with higher loads and engine speeds—have greater exhaust temperatures and run just as cleanly with four valves.) The move to a 3-valve-per-cylinder design did little to affect the performance of the engine, thanks in part to another new aspect of the V-6—its twin-plug ignition system.

The somewhat unattractive little black boxes mounted on each cam cover are ignition coils that provide power to a pair of sparkplugs per cylinder. The goal is to

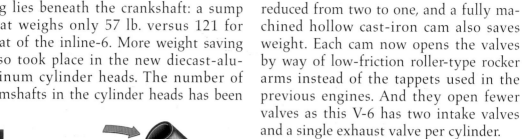

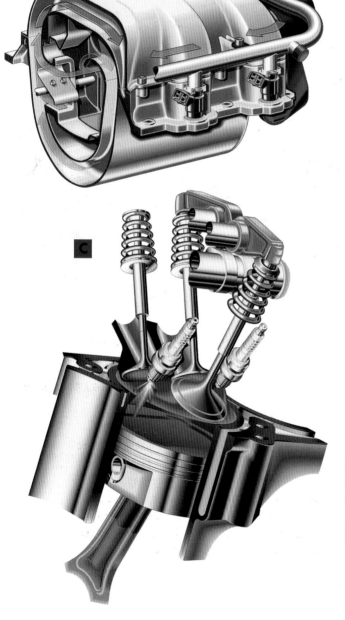

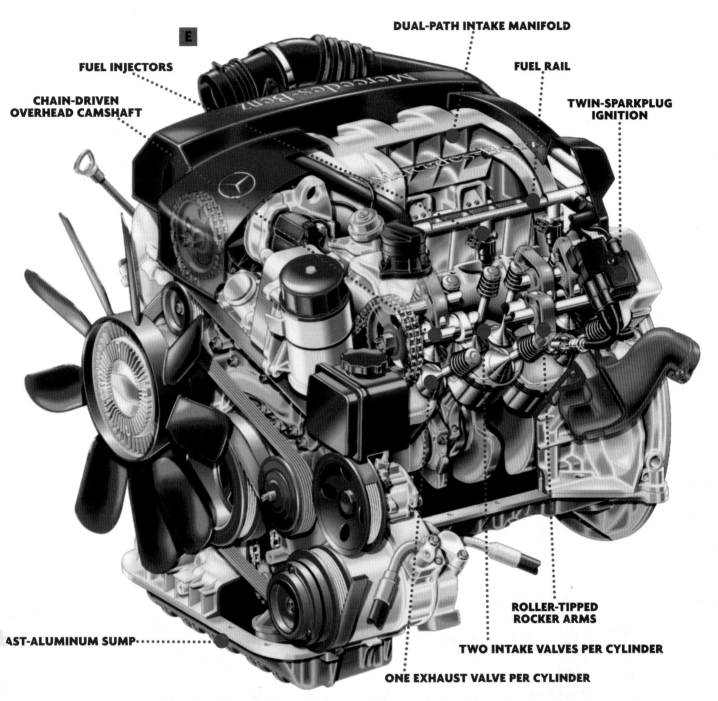

E

DUAL-PATH INTAKE MANIFOLD

FUEL INJECTORS

FUEL RAIL

CHAIN-DRIVEN OVERHEAD CAMSHAFT

TWIN-SPARKPLUG IGNITION

ROLLER-TIPPED ROCKER ARMS

AST-ALUMINUM SUMP

TWO INTAKE VALVES PER CYLINDER

ONE EXHAUST VALVE PER CYLINDER

B The new V-6 breathes through this dual-path intake manifold. An internal valve routes air to the long runners for low-rpm torque, and to a shorter path for better high-rpm power. **C** This image shows the M 112's 3-valve-per-cylinder layout (two intake, one exhaust), plus its roller-tipped rocker arms, narrow valve angle, compact combustion chamber and dual sparkplugs. **D** The aluminum block showcases the wonders of modern casting techniques. Note the liners, which are made of a specially coated light alloy for wear resistance. **E** The all-aluminum M 112 V-6 engine is 25 percent lighter, has lower emissions and is more fuel-efficient than the inline-6.

lower three things: fuel consumption, exhaust emissions and combustion noise. In the Mercedes V-6, the plugs don't fire simultaneously; they are phased to hold down the pressure gradients that affect combustion noise. Life of the platinum plugs is set at 100,000 miles.

Air reaches the cylinders via a variable-length intake manifold made of two diecast magnesium halves that have been bonded. When the automatically controlled flap in the manifold is closed, short-distance runners for each cylinder are used, improving high-rpm cylinder filling. When the flap is open, the engine has what Mercedes claims is the longest-path intake manifold in the world, which does wonders for low-rpm torque.

As with past Mercedes, the exhaust system contains catalytic converters and Lambda sensors, with double-walled sheet-steel exhaust manifolds. The air gap between the walls provides thermal insulation to keep exhaust gas temperature high and improve the efficiency of the catalytic converters during a cold start. The exhaust manifolds of the U.S. M-Class are made with a new technique in which lasers are used to weld the outer walls of the twin-skin manifold.

A master electronic engine-management system controls a long list of functions, such as opening and closing the intake manifold flap, metering the amount of fuel into the cylinders, firing the phased sparkplugs in correct sequence and continuously monitoring and diagnosing the engine's systems. Among the functions watched by the system is the engine-oil life, which is calculated and displayed on the instrument panel.

F

There's an interesting comparison between the inline-6 and the new V-6: Both have exactly the same 3199-cc displacement because they share identical bore and stroke of 89.9 mm x 84.0 mm. The engines even have the same compression ratio of 10.0:1 Though the V-6's horsepower is down to 215 bhp from 217, the torque is slightly up—229 lb.-ft. at 3000 versus the inline-6's 228 at 3750.

So why go to all the trouble of developing the new V-6? There is, as mentioned, the important matter of having a more compact engine for packaging and safety reasons. And this V-6 is 25 percent lighter than the straight-6, or about the same weight as the 4-cylinder used in export versions of the M-Class. While that torque number is only slightly better than before,

F The standard M-Class 5-speed automatic has a special program to ease "shift shock" in low range, and the ability to automatically select and hold 1st gear down steep off-road grades.

it is created 750 rpm lower and extends over a much wider rpm band, giving the engine greater driving flexibility. This last point makes both city and off-road driving much more enjoyable in the M-Class.

The combination of reduced engine friction, the dual ignition and improved exhaust recirculation produces an 8 percent improvement in fuel economy, giving the M-Class EPA fuel economy numbers that will likely beat its sport-utility competition. Also significantly lower are exhaust emissions. This is particularly important in the face of ever-tightening emissions laws around the world. With its phased dual ignition, secondary air injection and special exhaust manifolds, the 3.2-liter V-6 meets California's LEV (Low-Emissions Vehicle) standard, which is twice as difficult to meet as today's regulations. It helps, too, that the new V-6 is only in the beginning stages of its development life, with much more to come.

The second member of the new engine family, a 4.3-liter V-8, will eventually be used in the M-Class. And so will two other engines outside the U.S. The higher cost of fuel in Europe, Asia and Australia means that engine shipments from Germany to Tuscaloosa will also include a 2.3-liter inline-4 and a 2.7-liter inline-5 diesel.

Looking down on the shift lever of a U.S. M-Class, you will find that it reads P,R,N,D,4,3,2,1. Yes indeed, the ML320 will be available exclusively with the company's newest transmission, a 5-speed automatic. That extra gear translates into lower fuel consumption, greater reliability and improved comfort, the latter because of generally lower engine noise. Electronically controlled, the new 5-speed also has enhanced efficiency, with a lockup torque converter that can be activated in 3rd, 4th and 5th gears.

In these modern times, of course, the Mercedes automatic does more than just shift gears. It electronically interacts with other systems such as the traction control and anti-lock brakes. Known as the EGS system, the controller takes in all types of information, including engine data, the actions of the driver, barometric pressure and even if the M-Class is going up or down hill. From that information, the transmission can vary such factors as shift points and the firmness or softness of each gear change. All this is meant to optimize the vehicle's performance—even adapting to the driver's style—while also giving back the best in fuel economy.

Off-road drivers will particularly enjoy two features of the automatic. Typically, a sport utility with an automatic transmission will shift between gears in low range with enough force to slap you back in your seat. Mercedes' 5-speed has a special program that functions in low range to prevent that banging about. The other feature involves coming down a steep hill off-road. With the shift lever in "D" the ML320 gearbox senses the vehicle's attitude and remains in 1st gear unless the driver steps on the accelerator.

While this new combination of V-6 and 5-speed automatic transmission will also be available in the CLK and eventually a number of other Mercedes-Benz models, it is uniquely matched in the M-Class to an advanced drive system that effectively puts power to the ground, be it hot Texas pavement, the slippery roads of Washington's Olympic Peninsula, sandy gravel tracks in Arizona or a snowy highway in Vermont. Which brings us to the M-Class's new and different approach to 4-wheel drive.

Karl Benz and Gottlieb Daimler would have loved it, too.

COMING TO GRIPS

When the time came to develop a 4-wheel-drive system for its M-Class, Mercedes-Benz looked at those used by other sport-utility vehicles from around the world, and rejected them. Back at the drawing board, engineers in Germany applied modern electronics to classic principles and created a unique drive system for their new SUV.

For dozens of years, the term "4-wheel drive" brought with it images of expeditions plunging through uncharted jungles, farmers unloading feed in muddy fields or perhaps even a guy from the local gas station bolting a snow plow to the front of his pickup truck to earn a little extra money during winter. The accouterment often included bib overalls, well-used work gloves and plaid flannel shirts.

Plenty of men and women still earn a living with 4-wheel-drive workhorses, but there's also a new world of 4-wheel

drive. A world that starts one thinking about recreational activities such as skiing and fly-fishing. Then again, drivers have discovered the added safety and stability of having 4-wheel drive in foul weather, when the engine's power is being divided among four wheels rather than two.

It's not a new idea. The Dutch firm of Spyker amazed people at the 1903 Paris Salon automobile show with a 4-wheel-drive model, though it never went into production. Ettore Bugatti tried drive to all wheels in his fast-but-ferocious Type 53 Grand Prix car in the early Thirties, but technical limits of pieces such as the U-joints kept 4-wheel drive in the commercial and military vehicle arena.

Jeep, trying to take civilian advantage of its famous wartime design, continued developing postwar 4-wheel-drive vehicles. It required, however, rugged tenacity to drive those early models. Their suspensions were firm, their drive-trains were noisy and their interiors were agricultural at best. Worse yet, the vehicles weren't much to look at. If you wanted to use 4-wheel drive, you had to stop, put the vehicle in neutral, get out and lock the front wheel hubs (never fun in foul weather), get back in, select a 4-wheel drive range and then, finally, put the transmission in gear and drive away.

With the ever-increasing popularity and acceptance of sport-utility vehicles, however, came the financial impetus for manufacturers to make them much more comfortable and easier to use.

Today, there are three basic types of 4-wheel drive. Part-time is a system in which power is normally sent to either the front or rear wheels. When added traction is needed, you can flip a switch or pull a lever to engage the other axle, giving you 4-wheel drive. Typically, a low

gear range is available to make it easier to climb steep hills, power through deep sand or simply keep moving on low-traction surfaces. This is the simplest system and is generally found in pickup trucks and some sport utilities.

Full-time 4-wheel drive means power is always going forward and rearward. Con-

tained within a transfer case (that is connected to the transmission) is a center differential that apportions power between the front and rear wheels and also keeps the front and rear axles from binding up by allowing them to turn at different speeds. On many sport utilities with full-time 4wd, the center diff will automati-

cally send power to the axle getting the most traction. This action is "transparent" to the driver, meaning you just drive and it takes care of finding the most traction. As with the part-time system, this one has a low gear range.

All-wheel drive does much the same thing as full-time 4-wheel drive, but has no low range. Generally, all-wheel drive is found in cars such as the Mercedes-Benz 4Matic sedans and those ultraluxurious sport utilities that are least likely to venture off-road.

Problem is, that for all their axles, differentials and low ranges, many sport-utility vehicles don't really have true 4-wheel drive.

At this point we need to make a short foray to the technical side of automobiles and back to the aforementioned differentials. When power in a standard automobile goes to either the front or rear wheels, it is transferred to the road through the axle and tires. Driving straight down a dry road, each driven wheel is receiving half the available power.

Around corners, however, the inside wheel of the driven axle is traveling a tighter arc than the outside, so the outer wheel has to travel a greater distance to complete the turn. And if there is no way to let the wheels spin independently of one another, the driveline binds and the inside tire starts to howl as it's forced to rotate more than it needs to. A similar

▲What looks like a moguls run for the expert skier is actually a concrete-bump test section outside the Alabama factory. In this sequence, a disguised prototype is subjected to just about every uneven-traction scenario it might encounter. In frame 4, there's nearly three feet of air under that right front tire! ■Its 4-wheel-drive system functioning as designed, the Mercedes completes another run.

problem occurs when splitting the power between the front and rear axles of a sport-utility vehicle.

The device that prevents this binding is called a differential.

There's just one little problem. A differential always wants to route power along the path of least resistance. This is unimportant in most driving circumstances, but if you ever got caught with one wheel on dry pavement and the other on ice, power goes to the one that will spin the easiest, meaning you'll just be sitting there while the tire on ice merrily spins. This problem can be solved somewhat with a device called a limited-slip differential, though some of these are known to have a limited life.

Because a full-time 4-wheel-drive vehicle is not only sending power between two wheels on each axle, but also between axles, it has three differentials: one for each axle, and one in the transfer case, where power is split between the front and back axles.

Despite all these devices, however, if one wheel is on a patch of ice the vehicle will go nowhere, because the center diff, again, always sends power on the path of least resistance, which in this case is to the wheel on ice.

There is a solution to this. It is possible to lock the center differential to make certain equal power goes front and rear. But an important point to remember is that if one wheel on each axle can't get traction, the vehicle will still remain motionless.

Adding a locking differential to one axle, preferably the rear, helps your chances of getting unstuck, though this has to be reserved for low-speed travel because it creates the same problems, such as binding drivelines, that made differentials necessary in the first place.

Steering is also affected when a locked differential is installed in front.

There are a few vehicles, such as the Mercedes-Benz G-Wagen, in which you can lock the front, middle and rear differentials. This is the only true 4-wheel-drive system, and it will get you out of the most dire circumstances...usually at a low speed and only after the driver has had to stop and lock the "diffs."

Never a company to follow the lead of others, Mercedes-Benz thought long and hard about a true 4-wheel-drive system and chose a different route, applying modern electronics to create a unique, lightweight system for the M-Class.

The fundamentals are the same as those of most 4-wheel-drive sport utilities. Attached to the back of the ML320's 5-speed automatic transmission is a Borg Warner-produced transfer case. There's a differential in the transfer case that splits power 50 percent front/50 percent rear, using a chain to spin the driveshaft leading to the front differential. A normal driveshaft runs rearward to the back differential. But here's where things start getting unusual, because all three differentials are "open" or *non-locking*.

So what happens when an ML320's

THE M-CLASS 4WD SYSTEM: AN INSIDE LOOK

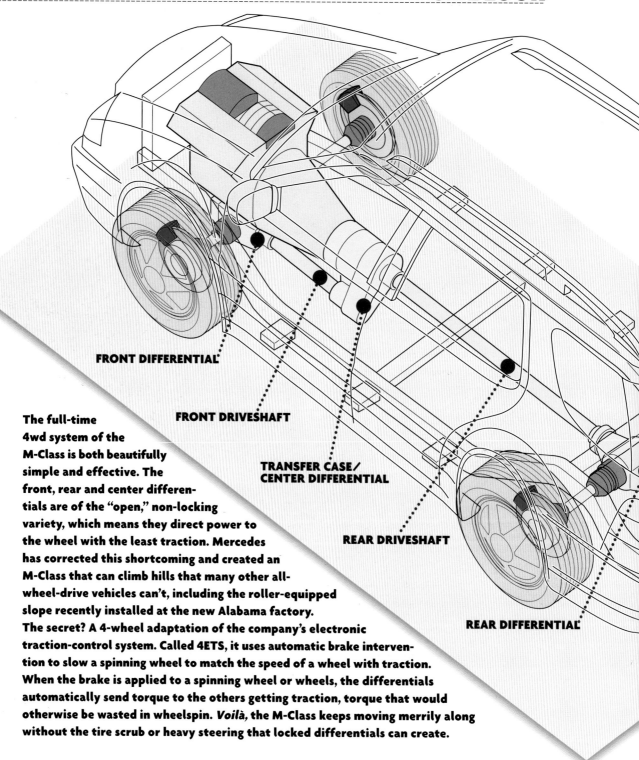

FRONT DIFFERENTIAL

FRONT DRIVESHAFT

**TRANSFER CASE/
CENTER DIFFERENTIAL**

REAR DRIVESHAFT

REAR DIFFERENTIAL

The full-time 4wd system of the M-Class is both beautifully simple and effective. The front, rear and center differentials are of the "open," non-locking variety, which means they direct power to the wheel with the least traction. Mercedes has corrected this shortcoming and created an M-Class that can climb hills that many other all-wheel-drive vehicles can't, including the roller-equipped slope recently installed at the new Alabama factory. The secret? A 4-wheel adaptation of the company's electronic traction-control system. Called 4ETS, it uses automatic brake intervention to slow a spinning wheel to match the speed of a wheel with traction. When the brake is applied to a spinning wheel or wheels, the differentials automatically send torque to the others getting traction, torque that would otherwise be wasted in wheelspin. *Voilà*, the M-Class keeps moving merrily along without the tire scrub or heavy steering that locked differentials can create.

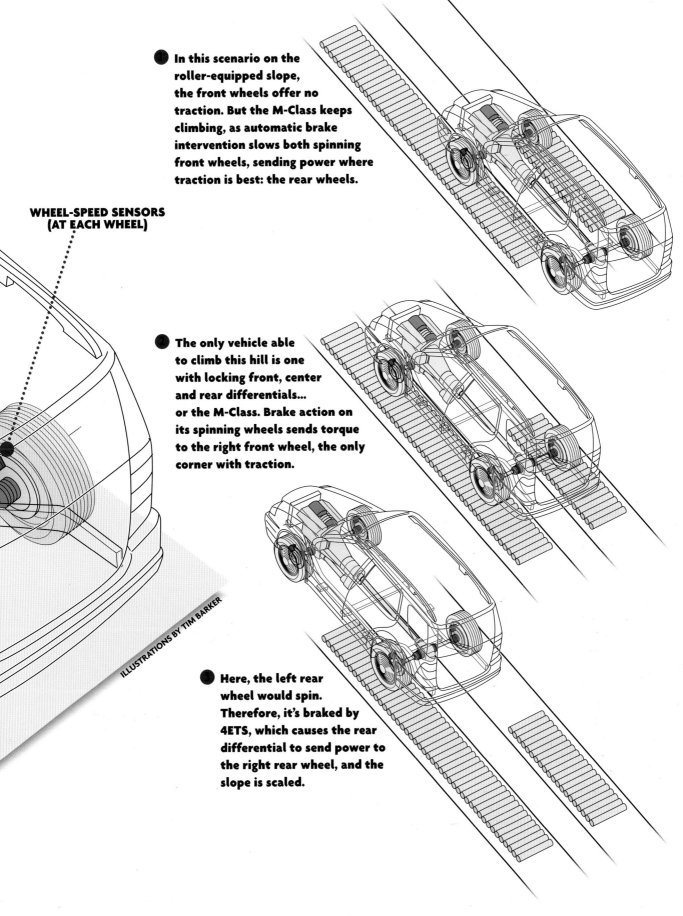

1 In this scenario on the roller-equipped slope, the front wheels offer no traction. But the M-Class keeps climbing, as automatic brake intervention slows both spinning front wheels, sending power where traction is best: the rear wheels.

WHEEL-SPEED SENSORS (AT EACH WHEEL)

2 The only vehicle able to climb this hill is one with locking front, center and rear differentials... or the M-Class. Brake action on its spinning wheels sends torque to the right front wheel, the only corner with traction.

ILLUSTRATIONS BY TIM BARKER

3 Here, the left rear wheel would spin. Therefore, it's braked by 4ETS, which causes the rear differential to send power to the right rear wheel, and the slope is scaled.

traction deteriorates on loose or slippery surfaces? Mercedes engineers took the company's electronic traction system (ETS), advanced it and applied it to all four wheels of the M-Class. This 4ETS is designed to maintain traction and stability under acceleration by applying braking action to a spinning wheel until its rotation matches that of the drive wheel with traction. In sedans that would mean only the rear wheels, but in the M-Class any of the four wheels that begins to spin is slowed by traction control.

Once a wheel on an M-Class starts to spin, sensors detect that slippage and begin to cycle pressure to that wheel's brake caliper to slow the rotation. At the same time, a warning light flashes on the instrument panel to let the driver know there's a traction problem.

As the spinning wheel or wheels are slowed by 4ETS, the available torque is routed back to the wheels with traction, increasing their pulling power. Even if three wheels are on ice and 4ETS is applying its traction control to each of them, the M-Class still will be able to get underway with no intervention from the driver, no flipping of switches, no locking of hubs, no special tricks. Just drive. Indeed, a far cry from the sport-utility vehicles that can easily get stuck with only one of their wheels on ice.

Incidentally, this system can kick in at speeds of up to 35 mph, and once activated, can keep working up to 50 mph. And anyone who has ever had to back up a driveway made slippery by snow, ice or wet leaves will be happy to know the M-Class system works in both forward and reverse gears.

For serious off-roaders, or to help those towing heavy loads, the M-Class's transfer case also offers a low range. While high range is a 1:1 ratio, pushing a "Low" button on the dash engages a 2.64:1 ratio, giving the Mercedes added "umph" for climbing steep hills with one of the slowest "creep" speeds on the SUV market. This also helps with engine braking when descending a hill. Don't forget that in this range the automatic transmission has its special softer-shift program for more comfortable driving, and will stay in 1st gear on a steep descent until the driver opens the throttle.

The beauty is that all this sophistication, all the electronic circuitry and wizardry, makes the M-Class system a true 4-wheel drive, and yet is completely automatic and invisible to the driver. And the gearbox and transfer case fluids never need to be changed or replenished. If the warning light didn't come on when the system was functioning, you'd never know the differentials, traction control, and controlling algorithms even existed.

Until, of course, you needed them to pull you quickly out of deep mud. ◄€

◄ A push of this console-mounted button engages low range, for maximum torque off-road.

CAMELS & FROZEN LAKES

Here was their assignment: Take these prototype sport-utility vehicles. Drive them as hard as possible. Try to break them. Put a million miles on them if needed, and make certain the production M-Class would be fit to carry the Mercedes-Benz star.

We were looking for photos that would document the development of the M-Class. Along the million or so miles racked up by Mercedes-Benz while putting its new sport utility through its paces, someone must have been taking photos. But we hadn't found any yet. Then, however, we went to the office of Karl-Heinz Richter, manager in the testing department. This office, in the Weisserth & Hieber complex, is where the new SUV was being turned from drawings and computer files into a real running vehicle.

Photographs? You need photographs? Richter laid down piles of pictures and began to name the places they'd been to test drive the M-Class: Tunisia, Sweden, Italy, France and then to America, to Death Valley, Denver, Laredo...quite a travelogue that racked up tens of thousands of miles.

Before anyone went anywhere, though—even before there were complete M-Class prototypes—the engines, transmissions, suspensions, cooling systems and such had to be bench tested at the factory. On devices such as dynamometers and special test rigs, drivetrains and individual pieces were cycled, abused, overheated and overcooled until they broke or proved worthy of being used on the new SUV.

As complete prototypes became available, full-vehicle testing began. Initial tests were done on the track at Untertürkheim, partially for the convenience of being near shops and garages in case of problems with the early vehicles, as well as for security reasons. This is also when wind-tunnel testing took place, but not just to calculate the aerodynamic efficien-

A The windmill and wide-open spaces might say Texas, but the camels show this test site to be Tunisia. **B** Dr. Gerhard Fritz, chief of the M-Class development, braves Sweden's cold to flash a smile. **C** The thin air of the Colorado Rockies tests the M-Class's breathing. Below, American mechanical engineer Mike Preissler at speed in Germany.

cy of the M-Class's exterior. Other tests measured the effectiveness of the windshield wipers at speed, and another simulated a downhill run to check if the brakes were getting sufficient cooling air.

There came a point, however, when the new baby had to leave home. Vehicles must live in the real world, so ultimately that's where they have to be tested. Making these trips even more crucial was the fact that the M-Class was a totally new type of automobile incorporating several original systems.

There was one danger: spies. A number of photographers make very good livings by tracking down and getting photos of prototype vehicles to show the world and competing automakers what these new machines look like. Spy methods involve stealth and patience, everything from hiding in the bushes along well-traveled test routes (in locales such as Death Valley) to knowing the names of the trucking companies that haul prototypes and following their transporters to testing locations.

A certain amount of exposure isn't all bad. It doesn't hurt to let the world know you are a progressive company, working

new products into the pipeline. But you don't necessarily want detailed pictures of the styling of a new car or sport-utility vehicle being splashed all over newspapers and magazines. Hence the camouflaging kits used on early prototypes to hide the final details of the design.

The point of the new SUV's worldwide trials? To take it to the extremes both dynamically and climatically, which explains a great deal about the development team's globetrotting itinerary.

France. Mt. Ventoux—which has been the site of famous competitive hillclimbs since the early years of the automobile—was used to test the cooling system of the M-Class. The 6-mile road has a tough 15-percent grade.

Italy. Here, the brakes were tested on the twisting Alpine roads. And at the famous Nardo circle track near Brindisi in southern Italy, the M-Class was driven at speeds up to 110 mph for 20 hours, stop-ping only for driver changes and fuel. In all, the M-Class logged more than 46,000 durability miles.

Tunisia. The Sahara desert provided 180 miles of dusty roads in the morning—a thorough mechanical check—plus another 180 in the afternoon. And in deep sand tests, the anti-lock brakes' special low-range program worked perfectly. What's more, there had to be a check of the 4-wheel-drive/ETS system, which requires wheelspin to activate. Would the wheelspin cause the tires to dig too deeply into the sand? It did not.

Sweden. In this northern country's frozen lakes and deadly cold, the M-Class stayed outside all night, and was then started in the morning of a midnight sun day, when there are only a few hours of daylight. How good was the heating system? How do the M-Class's fluids and parts—such as the shock absorbers and steering rack—react when it's 40 degrees

D The agility of a mountain goat? Perhaps not quite, but the M-Class is close. **E** Up to its wheel flanges in fine Tunisian sand, the M-Class undergoes tests of its 4-wheel-drive system. **F** Less rigorous, yet no less important testing at the German military test site. **G** On the lift for a chassis inspection. Below, the M-Class charges through Tuscaloosa's water trough during a leakage test.

below zero? On the rock-hard frozen lakes, how effective were the anti-lock brakes? And how did the revolutionary 4-wheel-drive system perform on hard-packed snow and ice? Magnificently.

America. The new home of the M-Class. Summer temperatures in Death Valley gave the cooling and air conditioning systems a serious workout. From there the M-Class was driven thousands of miles through the West to places such as Mt. Evans, Colorado, where the new V-6 had to deal with the highest road in the U.S., not to mention the thinnest air it probably ever will encounter.

This test took place in summer, 1995, when the testing team also headed south to Laredo, Texas, for high-speed lapping of a desert test track. Then the vehicles and crews went on to Houston and Corpus Christi for possibly the worst combination of heat and humidity in the country—95 percent humidity on a 100-degree day—where air conditioning and cooling systems never rest. Some emissions and fuel economy tests also took place in the Lone Star state.

And, finally, at home in Germany. On the same military base where the G-Wa-

The often bitter Swedish climate provides the raw materials for these ice houses as well as a grueling test environment for the M-Class—temperatures can plummet to -40 degrees Fahrenheit.

gen was tested, the M-Class was subjected to the abuse that can come only from repeated laps of a tough gravel circuit. Towing tests were conducted in the Swabian Alps, in which the M-Class pulled heavy trailers to assure that its drivetrain and cooling system will be up to the challenge of boaters and campers, who will buy the ML320 for its 5000-lb. towing capacity. And because a Mercedes must act like a Mercedes, prototypes were taken to the famous Nürburgring race track in the Eifel mountains for the equivalent of an 1800-mile road race.

If all this sounds like a great deal of fun, understand that the schedule was rugged. Participants were up early and ready for the road at 7:30 a.m. They drove all morning, stopping periodically to swap vehicles and information. And it wasn't a matter of driving along, looking at the countryside. Ask the engineers who were on these trips to describe what they saw of the passing landscape and their answers are short. They were too busy evaluating the M-Class, be it the drivetrain, suspension, steering or possibly the long-range comfort of the seats. Were the trim and other added pieces holding up well and remaining solidly attached despite the extreme cold, heat or vibration?

Because of the simultaneous engineering aspect of the M-Class, a trip might have included more than just engineers; it may have included others involved in the vehicle's development, such as the repre-

N On the highest paved road in the U.S.—on Mt. Evans, Colorado—an M-Class with disguised grille openings takes a well-deserved breather. **O** With significantly more oxygen available, an M-Class hurries around a high-speed oval in Laredo, Texas. **P** Arizona canyon walls make for a spectacular backdrop. **Q** Andreas Renschler, president of Mercedes-Benz U.S. International, Inc., surveys the Laredo landscape while Dr. Fritz prepares to take a picture.

sentatives of the suppliers who have done the final engineering of certain major components. These were not tourists, and it was far from being a joyride.

A short lunch break, then back on the road, driving and swapping vehicles, comparing ideas and answers, right up to the dinner hour. Oftentimes mechanics spend the evening hours fixing or modifying the test machines. Engineers finally got to break for dinner, but the work didn't end as problems and solutions were passed back and forth during the evening meal.

Dr. Gerhard Fritz, chief of M-Class development, says the evening discussions were invaluable. After all these miles together, the engineers became more than just business colleagues. They argued together, laughed, hunted for problems and offered solutions. All with one purpose: to make certain the new M-Class is fit to wear the Mercedes star.

Then they must get a good night's sleep, and be back on the road tomorrow.

NEW FACTORY, NEW METHODS

While Mercedes-Benz designers and development engineers were busy refining the M-Class in Germany and at test sites around the world, other experts in Alabama were laying the foundations for both the factory and the production system for their new SUV.

It's particularly impressive when seen for the first time at night. Heading west on Interstate 59—some 30 miles outside of Birmingham, Alabama, and 12 miles shy of Tuscaloosa—there are freeway signs that point out, "Mercedes Drive." To the left there is the slowly turning Mercedes-Benz star above the visitor and training center. Soon, the gleaming white factory appears through the blur of dark trees, looking too neat and clean to be an automobile manufacturing plant. And yet this is where Mercedes-Benz has built the lead factory in its plan to globalize and to learn.

One can't help but think it's a long way from the company's beginnings in Bad Cannstatt, Germany, 1886.

After the September 30, 1993, announcement that the state of Alabama and Tuscaloosa County had won the coveted Mercedes-Benz factory, things moved quickly. The following month, Reiner Görs took an initial look at his next architectural project. A 20-year veteran of designing and building in 13 countries, Görs had to situate the factory and visitor/training center on the 966-acre property and deal with the initial planning of everything from plant efficiency to the esthetics. This facility would be, after all, an important part of the transition from "Made in Germany" to "Made by Mercedes-Benz."

January, 1994: an important month for the factory. The renowned Detroit-based architectural and engineering design firm, Albert Kahn Associates (AKA), was hired.

Mercedes had vowed to use Alabama companies in all phases of this "learning field" facility, and several would be working with AKA. Greshman, Smith and Partners of Birmingham assumed responsibility for the combined visitor/training center. Grover Harrison Harrison, P.C., also of Birmingham, and McGiffert and Associates of Tuscaloosa also would be involved in the Mercedes project.

Fluor Daniel—which aided in the site selection search and is one of the world's

▲ **Birth of a factory: At left, cement trucks begin pouring the first of 40,000 cubic yards of concrete, an event not unnoticed by the media. Next, the elaborate girder trusswork starts to come together, piece by piece. Below, an aerial view of the nearly complete factory.**

The Birmingham News

Money

MARKETS/4-5B

Can't afford a business jet?
you can timeshare one/3B

Friday, October 20, 1995

GOP eases confrontational
stance on raising debt limit/2B

TODAY

Mercedes rolling on

Work on the sprawling Mercedes auto plant at Vance is more than 70 percent complete.

NEWS STAFF PHOTOS/JOE SONGER

Construction of Vance plant nearly three-fourths finished

By Stan Diel
News staff writer

Not to worry, says Dr. Herb Gzik, vice president for the financial color for the mammoth Mercedes-Benz plant under construction near Vance.

With work on the $500 million plant more than 70 percent complete, the lime green-colored layer of sheet metal covering much of the building's frame stands out like a German in Alabama.

But Gzik, a German and vice president for engineering the luxury automaker's plant, said the green exterior will be covered with insulation, then with another layer of sheet metal.

Just over two years ago Mercedes began construction of the plant, it had taken the exterior walls are going up...

Food W
strike
sched

By Roy Williams
News staff writer

A union represents bama in contract scheduled strike Representativ Workers Union for nearly a Food World e

The contra tended until reach agree president.

Unsatisf the union Oct. 28, plished a

The r in Alab Rober ance i ficult over

Wednesday
August 9
1995

Tourney an 'eye-opener' for V

B   **LOCAL/R**

GETTING CLO
EVERY DA

It's been a hectic, busy summ
Mercedes-Benz assembly plant
the facility gets closer to co

One of the most hectic work sites in Tuscaloosa County this summer has been the 966 acres where diverse crews are transforming a vast open space into an auto plant complex for Mercedes-Benz U.S. International.

August has found the site particularly busy. One reason is that at its halfway point in construction, the plant has lots of subcontractors doing their speciality, as well as installation crews getting plant machinery in place.

To help cope with the construction demands, work has been spread out with two overlapping shifts, said Herb Gzik, vice president for engineering. One reason for the additional shift is that some construction had been delayed by rain earlier this year.

"Now we have very, very hot weather," Gzik said. "It is impossible for some contractors to work below the roof or on top of the roof during the day," he said. "Also, "We really have a lot of people working on the site," he said. "For us, safety is on top of everything. Therefore, we have to make sure the different teams do not interfere with each other."

The earliest shifts start at 6 a.m. or 7 a.m. Second shifts begin in the afternoon and work into the evening, with the aid of flood lights or interior lights.

By late July, there were almost 400 people working on the site each day, plus others working on the highway interchange and other state road projects around the site.

"We will have, including Mercedes-Benz people, about 1,200 to 1,300 people in total in September," Gzik predicted. That level of construction employment will hold

---

THURSDAY, MARCH 2, 1995

The Tuscaloosa News

GOING UP

Workers erect the first steel beams Wednesday at the new Mercedes-Benz plant in Vance.

Staff/Amy Kilpatrick

Steel erected for auto plant

By MAX HEINE
Staff Writer

VANCE — "It is a great feeling," said Herb Gzik, vice president of engineering for Mercedes-Benz U.S. International, as he was watching across the lot.

German and American engineers who have been working in Germany, Gzik does to help Germany will come here to help build the with with the 25 team members hired in April this year.

Those plant members — the first production employees hired — will train for six months in Germany, plus also be productive as they they (PPS) shop, also known as the factory shop, has been under way for the concrete in the plant's shop.

Rising Wednesday, it took a large crane to situate two I-beam columns (or bolting onto concrete pads a few feet underground, the facility's first structural steel, looked like white beams relative to the warren 300 bolts Plan also

The columns and a truss that linked formed the first part of a wall for the PPS shop.

The cars built in the PPS will be hand-made, said Alfred Kuhne, a project engineer. The purpose is to check "manufacturability" — that is, whether the way of assembly and the ease of assembly will work. "You cannot test everything on a drawing," Kuhne said. After the PPS test production

Please see STEEL Page 8A

Mercedes presence brings many suppliers

By MAX HEINE
Staff Writer

TUSCALOOSA — If the local economy were a pinball game, the tilt light would be starting to flash.

In two years, Tuscaloosa's manufacturing sector has begun to lean further toward one side: automotive. While the bulk of job creation at Mercedes-Benz and its suppliers is still a year away, the extent of these coming attractions is pretty well known.

Following the Sept. 30, 1993, announcement that Mercedes would create 1,500 jobs, the dominoes have fallen as expected. Eight major supply contracts have been awarded for companies that are beginning to build new manufacturing facilities in Alabama — four of them in Tuscaloosa County and three more in west-central Alabama.

"We're extremely heavy toward the automotive sector now," said Dara Longgrear, executive director of the Tuscaloosa County Industrial Development Authority.

Tuscaloosa's manufacturing base has automotive component even with Mercedes-related business: Goodrich Tire Co., General Harrison Thermal Sy son Controls' plastic in operation employ some

3,000 people. That represents about 30 percent of the 10,400 manufacturing jobs in Tuscaloosa County during July.

Add the 2,100 jobs tied to Mercedes and its Tuscaloosa County-based suppliers — most of which have not been created yet — and automotive may account for roughly 40 percent at the 12,000 or more factory jobs that will exist in a year.

An undetermined number of other jobs directly or indirectly related to Mercedes manufacturing are expected to be created as warehousing operations spring up, Longgrear said. For example, Synchronous Industrial Services is building a large warehouse at Coton dale Industrial Park, where it will be well-positioned to serve Mercedes and its suppliers.

The increased automotive weighting creates the potential for Tuscaloosa being hurt by a cyclical downturn, Longgrear said, but the IDA is aiming to tip the scales back.

"We will continue to try to diversify our economy and try to recruit industry away from the automotive industry," he said. "We'll also be focusing on the more value-added aspect of the automotive industry — this would include engineering services and tool and die operations.

Even though automotive may dominate local manufacturing, factory jobs account f

---

Mercedes-Benz Suppliers map

DUNLOP TIRE
Will supply tire
from existing pla

HUNTSVILLE

JOHNSON CONTROLS
seating systems
and headliners
• $15 million
• 125 jobs

REHAU
bumpers
• $10 million
• 40 jobs

DELPHI PACKARD
ELECTRICAL SYSTEMS
dashboards
• $6 million
• 100 jobs

CULLMAN

MERCEDES-BENZ
all-activity vehicles
• $535 million
• 1,500 jobs

OGIHARA AMERICA
doors, fenders, hoods
• $70 million
• 130 jobs

ZF INDUSTRIES
axle systems
• $75 million
• 200 jobs

BIRMINGHAM

TUSCALOOSA VANCE

BECKER GROUP
door trim and
sidewall trim panels
• $15 million
• 200 jobs

TUSCALOOSA

T&WA Inc.
tire and wheel assemblies
• $9 million
• 25-200 jobs

PRATTVILLE

ARKAY PLASTIC
plastic parts
• $7 million
• 130 jobs

BOLIGEE

Mercedes-B
Suppliers

county. Mining and construction provide 7,000 jobs, and the broad category of "service producing" encompasses 54,000 jobs.

Mercedes is furth
cal operation than a
yet it has only 175 p
Please see SUPPLIE

SUPPLIERS

Continued from Page 1E

jected 1,500 based here. Another 150 work in Stuttgart, Germany, said spokeswoman Linda Paulmeno.

"The majority of the recruitment will occur in '96 and '97," she said.

The creation of high-paying automotive jobs is about to put pressure on existing employers, said Dick Johnson, chairman of The Chamber of Commerce of West Alabama. It is likely to affect the entire spectrum of employers as skilled workers get the new jobs, creating vacancies that will be filled by those of lesser skills, he said.

"One of the things we can do is make sure that people in the Southeast especially, and perhaps throughout the country, know that there are job opportunities here for qualified people," Johnson said. Consequently, the chamber may coordinate "some sort of marketing effort to make sure people know we're open for business."

Dave Kauppila, manager of the Delphi Harrison plant and head of the chamber's existing industry task force, is working on that project, Johnson said.

So far the economic impact from Mercedes "seems to be right in line with what people were thinking," Johnson said. Longgrear agreed.

The impact
whelmed my
said. "We evalu
rectly early on,
as many as 10 s
turing plants, t
ing to shake ou

"Even thou
and internation
be significant,
mated that," h
example, he
September "the
that really we
prior to the a
ing clients as
toward having
we have clien

The Tuscaloosa News

B

ant should be tourism hot spot

Crowd pleasers

By MAX HEINE
Staff Writer

Staff/Neil Brake

top engineering and construction firms—was named to manage the building of Mercedes' landmark facility. Contracts were let for the planning and creation of the various work stations and assembly lines inside the factory. It was an international group. Durr Industries of Germany (via Detroit) would do the paint shop with its dip tanks and paint booths. The German firm, Kuka/Edag, got the nod to lay out and install the welding machines of the body shop. And Mitsubishi/Chiyoda's Detroit office was chosen to design and install the final assembly line, where all the parts would finally become M-Classes. At the time, Herbert Gzik, who then headed engineering for what was still called the Mercedes-Benz Project, explained why these firms were chosen: "They share our vision for innovation and lean production. With this team we were able to draw from American, German and Japanese cultures and expertise in building this world-class automotive facility. We were drawing the best from the best."

This same philosophy of diversity drove the early hiring of those who would set up and operate the M-Class factory, people who brought with them the accumulated experience of years with Ford, General Motors, the U.S. operations of Toyota and Nissan, and, of course, Mercedes-Benz. In early May, the initial group of executives who would work with project leader Andreas Renschler was announced. Matthias Ibach, then 36, was part of the program from its beginnings in Germany. He would bring his expertise in plant controlling and strategic planning to the job of financial con-

■ Needless to say, word of the factory's progress was front-page news in local papers.

111

C

trol of the learning field. William Taylor, 44, was to head all production, drawing on his years as general manager of Toyota's manufacturing facility in Canada and 18 years with Ford. Dr. Gerhard Fritz, 49, would lead the design and development of the vehicle.

Bob Birch, 48, had 12 years with Nissan's U.S. auto factory and experience with GM that would serve him well with the purchasing and logistics. Roland Folger, 34, brought the perspective of his years working for Mercedes in the U.S., Germany and Southeast Asia to the job of marketing and service. Emmett Meyer, 51, had worked with Daimler-Benz's AEG-Westinghouse Transportation subsidiary prior to taking the human resources job at Tuscaloosa. Herbert Gzik, 39, who brought with him experience in automation and robotics, would head up engineering.

Run down the list of others who would head key departments and you'll find a

D

similar variety of experience. Such as Alan Arrasmith, manager of the body shop—he helped start the Subaru-Isuzu factory in Indiana, and trained with Nissan in Japan. Bill Bugg was involved in the opening of Toyota's Camry factory in Georgetown, Kentucky. And the list goes on. Mercedes made a point of hiring people with different experiences and points of view, then letting them discuss, even argue among themselves about how best to arrange the production system at Tuscaloosa. All the better to learn.

Experts deciding how the plant would be laid out knew it had to be unlike other Mercedes-Benz factories. Whereas the Mercedes Sindelfingen or Bremen factories stamp steel sheet into body panels and receive the thousands of parts that become a Mercedes, Tuscaloosa would be different. Sheet metal pieces already shaped into their final form and large subassemblies, such as completed seats, suspension systems and entire dashboards, would be delivered by suppliers for final assembly. This factory would be much more compact than the others. Body shop and paint lines that might be laid out in a straight line in many factories were folded into tight esses in the new Mercedes plant.

First, however, there had to be a plant to contain this innovative production system. Ground was broken on May 4, 1994, with Andreas Renschler, then-Alabama gover-

nor Jim Folsom and Dr. Dieter Zetsche, deputy board member from Mercedes in Germany, doing the honors with shovels. Zetsche declared, "We are planting the seed for what will become a cornerstone of how Mercedes-Benz will operate in the future on a worldwide basis." Also taking a turn with the shovels were students from 12 Tuscaloosa area schools, representing the "seeds of the future." Elmer Harris, who heads the Alabama Power Company, was there too. Says Elmer: "The entire state felt pride to have such an outstanding car company in Alabama."

Earth-moving equipment was fired up and started rearranging the landscape off Interstate 59/20 in what is officially Vance, Alabama, a small town that had been bypassed by the interstate. As construction progressed, Mercedes followed

■With its sine-curve roof and slowly rotating Mercedes star, this impressive structure doubles as a visitor center and training facility. The manufacturing plant is in the background.
■The management team of the M-Class, from left to right: Dr. Gerhard Fritz-V.P. Development, William Taylor-V.P. Operations, Roland Folger-V.P. Strategic Marketing & Service, Matthias Ibach-V.P. Finance & Controlling, Herbert Gzik-V.P. Engineering, Robert Birch-V.P. Purchasing & Logistics and Emmett Meyer-V.P. Human Resources & Administration. Seated: Andreas Renschler-President & CEO.
■Gracing the factory's lobby is an early example of a Daimler motorcoach.

through on its promise to support the local economy. Four of the eight consulting firms for the visitor/training center were minority/African-American companies, while a fifth was a minority/women company. The list of contractors for the manufacturing plant had names such as Dunn Construction Company of Birmingham, Alabama Gate City Steel of Birmingham, TTL, Inc. of Tuscaloosa and Meador Contracting Company of Mobile, which is owned by a woman. By December, 1994, the first of the 40,000 cubic yards of concrete needed for the factory was being poured. By then, what had been called Mercedes-Benz Project, Inc. finally had a permanent name, Mercedes-Benz U.S. International, Inc.

MBUSI, as it's commonly called, was hiring more and more employees, who were now filling a series of temporary buildings on the factory site. Next to them, structural steel was going up, and the finishing touches were completed during the 18 months between early 1995 and mid 1996. That summer of 1996, Mercedes employees were finally able to move out of their cramped temporary quarters into their shiny new building.

Architect Reiner Görs wanted employees to enjoy being in the building, explaining, "People should come into the factory and feel that Mercedes cares. They are our people and they should like the building. It's their working place and they will spend a great deal of time here, so I

F As trainees look on, some of the 70 German trainers demonstrate welding techniques.
G Workers inspect the finish on an M-Class hatch in the virtually dust-free paint department.

tried to give them an atmosphere that is light and clean."

In an architectural style that is European with an American touch, the factory is designed so that both local workers and those on assignment from Germany will feel at home. You enter a low, comfortable lobby and a few steps take you into a small assembly hall that acts as an orientation center, a place for meeting visitors and, in general, a central point of communication. Off to the right is the cafeteria, while straight ahead you can see painted M-Class bodies being shuttled from the paint shop to final assembly.

Upstairs are administrative offices in an open plan in which departments are separated by meeting rooms that have enough glass to keep them from ruining the spacious feel. More second-story offices extend into the production area over the locker rooms, making this a central point for engineers as well as workers. Says Görs: "The logistics people are able to look down to the logistics area, the paint shop people look down to the paint shop and the assembly people can observe their area as well. They are where they have to be to see what is going on and have the shortest route to their departments."

Görs feels landscaping of the factory grounds is important, so planting grass was an early priority, but not just for es-

thetic reasons. The famous red clay of the South will, when wet, suck the boots right off your feet. And when dry it creates an insidiously pervasive dust. Even the fine filters of the paint department couldn't rid the air of dust, so that section of the factory has been pressurized to keep the dirt out.

At several special areas in and around the plant, tall fences with special signs create free-trade zones. Because of an arrangement that Mercedes has made with U.S. Customs, materials brought into the factory from overseas won't be charged a duty if they are installed on a vehicle that will be exported.

Whereas the factory had to be fairly straightforward, Görs used more imagination for the building that houses the visitor/training center. Topped by the three-pointed star, this structure has an undulating roof that's reminiscent of Alabama's rolling hills or perhaps even the gullwing doors of a Mercedes-Benz 300SL from the Fifties.

Most of the floorspace—almost 100,000 square feet—of this dual-purpose building is devoted to a training center where new assembly line workers hone their skills before moving over to the factory. The other purpose of the center is to greet visitors and give them a bit of background about Mercedes-Benz. This area is

run by Paige Moreland, a native Alabaman with a museum background. Displays educate visitors about Mercedes' history, its long record of safety and technological advances, how it designs automobiles, the company's rich racing history and how Mercedes has become a global company. This last point is no small matter, given Tuscaloosa's role.

For all the activity taking place at its new factory, Mercedes-Benz wasn't the only company outfitting a new facility in the Tuscaloosa-Birmingham area. A conventional auto plant may have a list of as many as 500 suppliers. Under the Tuscaloosa learning field experiment, Mercedes' tally stops at 65, and it's an international list with names such as Nippondenso, Filtros Mann S.A., Eberspaecher/Calsonic, and one that's long

been famous in the North American auto industry, Canada's The Budd Company. Of great importance to Alabama, however, is that the large number of supplier jobs brought to the state by Mercedes' "just-in-time" production system requires local manufacturing. In the immediate Tuscaloosa area, the list of those firms supporting Mercedes includes among others, Delphi Packard Electrical Systems (100 jobs), ZF Industries (200) and the Becker Group (200). Birmingham has 130 jobs at Ogihara America, Rehau supplies bumpers and 40 jobs in the town of Cullman, while Arkay Plastics hired 130 people to work in its Autuga plant.

Elmer Harris, president and CEO of Alabama Power Company, sees the influence of the new factory going beyond just those companies. "I think that in 10 years

H

or less you will see the entire corridor from Tuscaloosa to Birmingham close in with economic activities, including industrial, commercial and, of course, residential areas." In the process, he adds, it will bring all the local communities closer together, something that wouldn't have happened without Mercedes-Benz.

While the building of its physical plant was MBUSI's outward sign of progress, there was also a great deal of work taking place behind the scenes. As certainly as development engineers were driving M-Class prototypes through Tunisian desert sands and across frozen Swedish lakes, the other team members were building additional foundations for the project's success. For example, Matthias Ibach, who handles money matters for the Tuscaloosa factory, had to develop a lean financial system. Says Ibach: "We had a chance to reinvent the financial wheel. Our overall philosophy of finance and accounting is to be as lean as possible."

There were also situations in which an established system proved best. After careful study, it was decided that MBUSI shouldn't deal with currency management. To have accountants in Alabama working with the Japanese yen, Italian lira and French franc didn't make sense when there was a department in Germany set up to deal with that situation. As a result, MBUSI buys engines and transmissions from Mercedes in Germany and sells vehicles back to them, all with dollars. Meanwhile, invoicing and collecting various monies from around the world is handled at the headquarters in Germany.

Ibach points out that the challenges don't end with the debut of the M-Class, saying that, "The future challenge will be to optimize profit by reducing costs not only here in Tuscaloosa, but also at our systems suppliers." There is also the profit potential in learning to balance M-Class vehicle sales worldwide: "To sell cars to the markets where you get, depending on competitive pricing and development of the exchange rates, the very best profit. This is the challenge, to optimize profits through shifting cars around the world. By shifting around 10 to 15 percent of our production volume we can make a nice impact on profit."

With the spanking-new Vance factory as a backdrop, an M-Class ascends one of the test track's hills... ...and from an even higher perspective, a shot of the factory and test track.

OPERATING ON THE EDGE

Just developing a new type of vehicle is hard enough. And building it in a country far from the home market only adds to the challenge. To do this, Mercedes will be using a different, leaner method of manufacturing.

When an automaker decides it should build an automobile in a different country, it typically transplants what it is successfully doing at home to the new location. That, however, wasn't enough of a challenge for the new Mercedes. For its brand-new M-Class, it needed to develop a better way of building the vehicle.

This is not a transplant operation like Nissan's or Toyota's American plants, where the complete manufacturing, production, logistics and people systems have been shipped over from Japan.

Mercedes-Benz wanted things to be different; it wanted an innovative new system that would foster the company's new global strategy.

Change is, of course, one of the objectives in creating the learning field in Tuscaloosa. In the production system, this means altering the way automobiles are manufactured. Henry Ford's Rouge River factory in Detroit was the ultimate example of the old ways, literally taking iron ore in at one end and sending completed cars out the other. Famous factories, such as Mercedes' Sindelfingen plant in Germany, start with huge rolls of sheet steel and seemingly endless pallets of parts that are crafted and assembled into finished automobiles. Judging by Mercedes-Benz's reputation for building fine automobiles, that system has worked very well for decades. Classic Mercedes cars from the Thirties are singled out at vintage shows for having handcrafted Sindelfingen bodies, while modern Mercedes are renowned for their fine quality. Evidence, however, points to a need for a changed system.

Until now, a company would design a new automobile, order basic materials and pieces, and then manufacture them into a complete car. Under the new methodology, the company still does the basic design, but it simultaneously engineers the vehicle with suppliers who take on responsibility for the final design of their part for the new car. Bob Birch, who heads the complex logistical department at Mercedes, explains: "As the M-Class was being created in Germany, Ogihara America, which stamps out most of the exterior sheet metal, sent engineers to Germany to sit in our offices and run CAD systems to design the product. They also sat in our function groups and made suggestions like, 'If you change this from a right angle to an arc, it will be easier for us to make the tool, and we can save some money.'" Other suppliers provided similar input, such as ZF Industries with the axles, while Delphi Packard Electrical Systems worked on the final details of the complex "cockpit" (dashboard) it produces for the Mercedes sport-utility vehicle.

Although building a part for the M-Class required early involvement and a strong financial commitment from the supplier, it is well worth their while. A part that costs Mercedes $100 per car is equal to a $60 million contract over the life cycle of the M-Class. Companies then build the parts and deliver them to the Tuscaloosa factory not as thousands of big and little pieces, but as subassemblies. Sometimes they are basic elements, like unpainted full-side body stampings with a few pieces already welded into place. Several are quite complex, such as ZF's axles and Delphi's cockpit.

Big or small, none of the parts are delivered to Mercedes warehouses where they can be stored and used as needed, but are unloaded directly into the factory where they quickly become part of the assembly system. This is the complex "just-in-time" production system. Birch says that once an M-Class body has been assembled and painted, "We have an electronic broadcast system to our suppliers, who have their plants nearby, to tell them what we need. They have a set amount of time to build their part, put it on a truck and get it to our production line. This is such a tight system that when the vehicle is being put together and painted, the seats don't even exist yet.

"And it isn't only 'just-in-time,' it's also in sequence. We broadcast that a vehicle, say, will receive a sand-colored leather interior and certain options, such as the Bose stereo. Then we inform them of the content of the next vehicle and so on. The parts are built in that order and their trucks have conveyors in them to ensure they are brought to the line in the correct order.

"This building, like any automaker's assembly plant, is expensive. Any square foot you can cut out of warehouse space is a considerable savings in capital investment. Our general suppliers' buildings aren't nearly as costly as this factory. Our plant is a million square feet, and by automobile standards that's small. As these processes get put into place, on into the year 2000, factories will grow smaller, not bigger, because they're just too expensive."

Just as you won't see great storehouses of parts waiting to be put into the assembly system, you won't see small parking lots—"buffers" in production jargon—of painted bodies or partially assembled M-Classes, waiting to be fed into the next step in the process. There is not enough space and there is not enough time. William Taylor, vice president of operations at MBUSI in Tuscaloosa, explains: "Our buffers are small because this creates a challenge, it makes you operate on a different level, and you operate on the edge all the time…you cannot learn unless you're on the edge." And learning is, of course, one of the purposes of the Alabama factory. "You learn," Taylor continues, "through problems. The countermeasure is not to increase the buffer, but to solve the problems."

As suppliers' parts are strategically fed into the assembly process, the human element comes into play. And the safety of Mercedes-Benz workers is considered as crucial as the safety of any person riding in a Mercedes-Benz vehicle. Unlike some highly automated factories, Mercedes' Tuscaloosa plant has a minimal number of robots, and they are there for safety reasons when work such as major body welding is done, and for extreme precision when, for example, the glue for the M-Class windshields is applied.

Tuscaloosa's human involvement is somewhat different than in Mercedes' German factories. In Germany, skilled craftsmen assemble the automobiles. In Tuscaloosa, workers who don't necessarily have automotive factory experience are taught a standard, easily repeatable job. With the proper parts and an intelligent, motivated work force, says Taylor, vehicles can be built with the quality expected from Mercedes-Benz. It's a different

approach than in the past, and it's necessary because, Taylor adds, "The customers demand—they don't ask for, they demand—a high level of quality."

When this new system is up to speed and running smoothly, two shifts of these new Mercedes-Benz workers will be dependably building as many as 270 M-Class sport-utility vehicles each day.

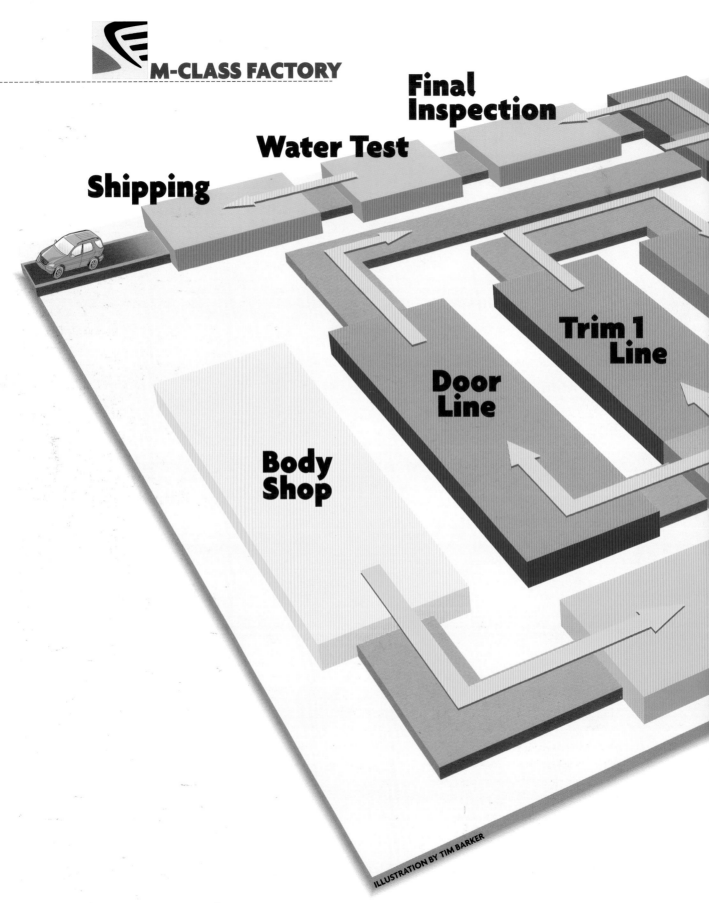

M-CLASS FACTORY

Final Inspection

Water Test

Shipping

Trim 1 Line

Door Line

Body Shop

ILLUSTRATION BY TIM BARKER

122

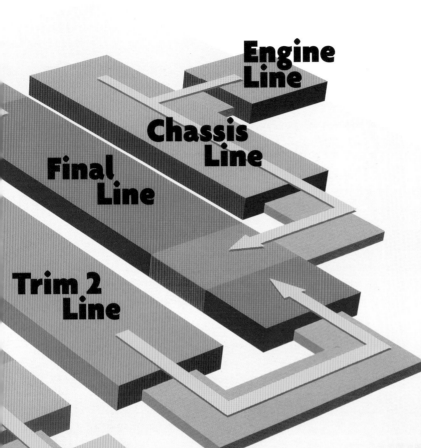

Engine Line

Chassis Line

Final Line

Trim 2 Line

Paint Shop

At Mercedes' "just-in-time" Tuscaloosa factory*, the body and chassis begin life at separate stations. After painting, the body moves to the Trim Line, where the doors are removed. The body continues down the Trim Line while the doors are fitted with components on the Door Line. The body moves from the Trim Line to the Final Line, where it mates to a chassis already fitted with driveline and suspension components. Then the doors are refitted. From there, the M-Class goes to Final Inspection, a water test and shipping. The following pages show the construction of an M-Class from sheet metal to finished product.

*Illustration is a representation of the factory and not to scale.

Factory Facts...

- **Length of assembly line:**
  1.2 kilometers (3937 ft)
  (four times the height of the Eiffel Tower)
  (26 times the height of the Statue of Liberty)

- **Number of welds done in body shop:**
  1520

- **Number of stations on assembly line:**
  123

- **Maximum factory output:**
  per year: 70,000
  per day: 270
  per hour: 16

- **Assembly time from start to finish:**
  10.5 hours

- **Number of body colors:**
  10

- **Total number of parts on vehicle:**
  14,000

- **Total number of parts
  (as delivered by suppliers—
  most are subassemblies of many parts):**
  1195

- **Distance to closest supplier:**
  8 miles DELPHI (Cottonwood, Alabama)

- **Distance to farthest supplier:**
  5600 miles Daimler-Benz AG (Stuttgart, Germany)

- **Number of team members involved in actual assembly:**
  January 1997: 127 (not including body and paint)

- **Area of plant:**
  1 million square feet

THE BODY SHOP

Our photographic trip through the M-Class factory will show how one of the new Mercedes sport-utility machines is assembled. It begins in the Body Shop with racks of sheet metal parts from Ogihara America Corporation and South Charleston Stamping & Manufacturing. Under the "just-in-time" system, pieces are delivered with many smaller reinforcements and attachments welded into place. Doors are received already built-up, ready to be fitted. At the Tuscaloosa factory, major parts are further welded together by hand and robot. The basic form of the M-Class emerges as it passes down the Body Shop line, headed next for the Paint Shop.

Every station in the factory, right through to the Final Inspection, is created so its task can be done in 3.6 minutes, which equates to 135 vehicles per shift, with two shifts per day.

The safety of those who own a Mercedes is crucial in the vehicle's design, and worker safety is a cornerstone of the production system in Tuscaloosa.

THE PAINT SHOP

The second major stop for an M-Class is the Paint Shop, which is sealed off from the rest of the factory, even to the point of being pressurized to keep dust and other impurities out.

The first step in the paint process is a thorough cleaning of the bare M-Class, which has just arrived from the Body Shop. This phosphate pretreatment is followed by what's called the e-coat, a primer treatment that greatly inhibits corrosion. After the e-coat is baked, the body is cooled and sanded before the seams and underbody are coated with a viscous PVC sealant, again to prevent rusting. This coating is also baked, then cooled, and the body then gets another primer coat—light or dark, depending on the final paint color— that is also baked.

The M-Class's primer coat is sanded and the vehicle finally gets its base coat of colored paint. A trip through an infrared oven "flashes" out any moisture in the water-based paint, which is then covered by a clear coat that gives the M-Class its final shine. After a wax coating to seal the nooks and crannies of the body, the Mercedes SUV enters a "selectivity bank," ready for assembly.

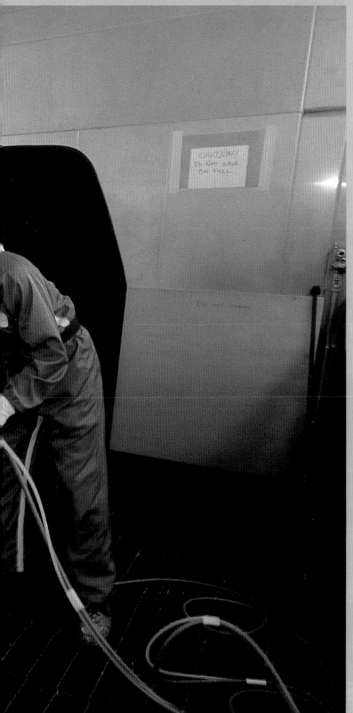

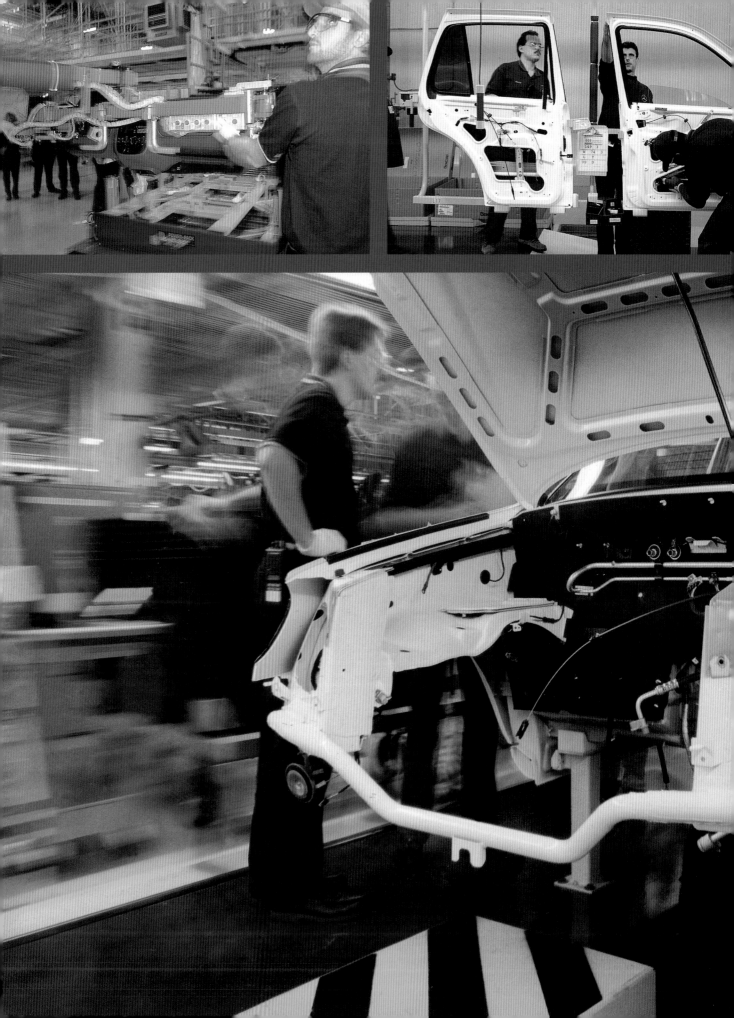

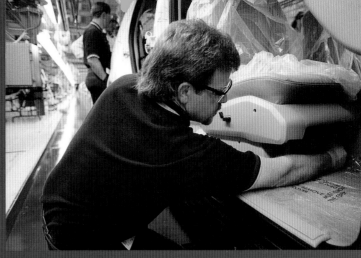

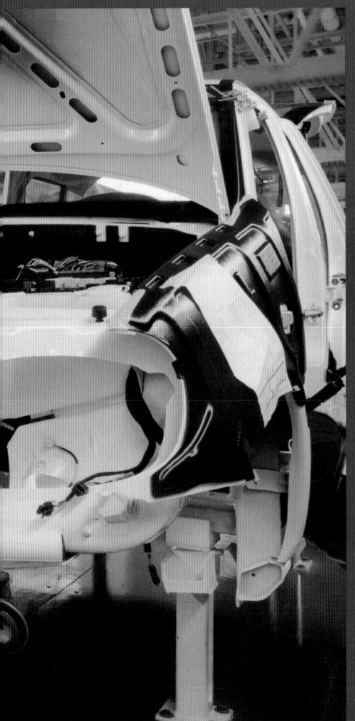

THE TRIM LINES

Each freshly painted M-Class body is transferred along an elevated line. From the Paint Shop, it glides behind the tall glass windows of the communications area near the factory lobby, where team members and visitors can see the bodies being moved to the Trim Line.

Once on the line, the doors are removed from the body and sent to their own line to have items added, such as the radio speakers and door panels. When finished, these doors will be reunited with their M-Class body near the end of the assembly process.

Along the two Trim Lines, hundreds of pieces are installed, everything from the wiring harness to the carpeting. The dashboard or "cockpit" is perhaps the most complex subsystem in the vehicle, and like all subassemblies— i.e., the seats, axle subframes and pedal assemblies—it is built in a supplier's factory and delivered exactly when it's needed to go into a specific M-Class. In one of the few automated robot stations in the factory, the windshield glue is applied prior to hand fitting.

Looking more and more like a real vehicle, the painted and partially trimmed M-Class body heads for its "marriage" with the chassis.

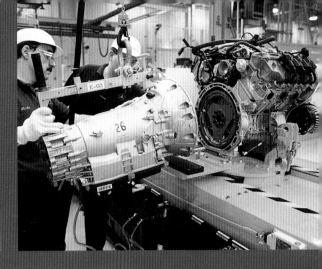

THE CHASSIS LINE

While the M-Class body is being fitted with hundreds of parts, the chassis is being finished on the Chassis Line. This procedure begins with the bare frame, which is set on a carrier and is mated with its axles and Mercedes' unique independent suspension. The anti-lock brake system is also added as the chassis heads for a T-junction on the assembly line.

On the extension known as the Engine Line, the German-made engines and 5-speed transmissions are joined with their U.S.-sourced transfer cases. Parts such as the air conditioning compressor and exhaust manifolds are added, and then this driveline is sent over to the Chassis Line to be installed in a frame. As more pieces are added—driveshafts, fuel tank, spare tire, etc.—the chassis looks like a huge go-kart that needs only a seat and tires to be driven away.

Now the chassis is ready to be joined to the body.

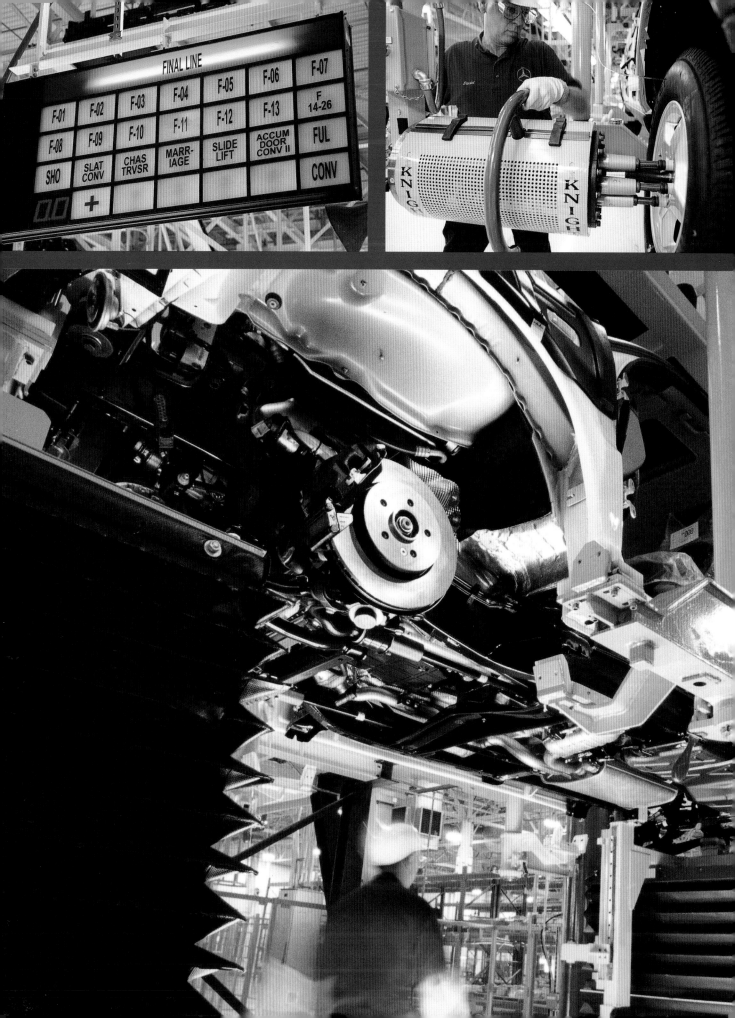

THE FINAL LINE

Here's where the marriage of body and chassis takes place. The body is fitted onto 10 rubber mounts as it is mated to the freshly finished chassis. Much of the remaining work involves systems that are shared by both body and chassis, such as the installation of steering and air conditioning components. Once the wheels and necessary fluids have been added, the M-Class is almost finished.

Throughout the entire production process, team members are allotted 3.6 minutes to complete each assigned task. Team members at MBUSI work with a standard method and procedure when performing their tasks. These standards help team members assemble the M-Class SUVs to the company's traditionally high standards.

If a problem occurs at a station, a team member can pull a line stop cord and a team leader comes to help. If this difficulty isn't resolved, the line can be stopped at the end of the 3.6-minute cycle. Solving the root cause of problems is a factor built into the Mercedes system, where continuous improvement occurs because all team members are encouraged to continually improve the means of accomplishing their tasks.

FINAL INSPECTION

Just because an M-Class now looks finished and even runs under its own power doesn't mean Mercedes is done with it. There are still a few things that need adjustment, such as the alignment and pedal pressures.

In the above photos, the M-Class is driven over bumps to settle its suspension, tested for power output on a dynamometer, sprayed with water to look for leaks and, finally, checked for quality in the best way possible—by an MBUSI team member.

After a small sampling is subjected to track testing and additional quality checks, a protective covering is applied to the hood and roof to prevent any shipping damage. About half the vehicles are headed for Mercedes-Benz of North America dealers; at this point their price stickers are applied and the new M-Classes are driven onto transporters for distribution around the U.S.

The other half of production is planned for dealers in other parts of the world. These M-Class vehicles, some of which will have a V-6, 4-cylinder or diesel engine and right-hand drive, are loaded and trucked to either Jacksonville, Florida, or Brunswick, Georgia, to be shipped to their final destination, whether the buyer lives in Germany, Australia, Japan or anywhere else in the world.

PEOPLE POWER

Countless new parts and processes are needed to build the new M-Class in Tuscaloosa County. But in the end, it's the people who are most important, and they are a truly fascinating mix of American and German cultures.

Two different types of employees were needed for the Tuscaloosa factory: executives with invaluable experience in "just-in-time" production, and production and maintenance people who could be trained to repeatably and dependably build the M-Class to Mercedes-Benz's historically high standards.

Emmett Meyer, the vice president of Human Resources at Tuscaloosa, was closely involved in hiring. When it came to choosing people who would lead the various departments, Meyer explains: "We looked at the experiences of transplant companies in the U.S., even though we are specifically not a transplant. Some companies recruited from only one automaker. The advantage is

A

that all these new hires think alike…but that's also the disadvantage.

"So we decided to hire people from various companies who had particular areas of expertise that were worthy of looking at in more detail. This enabled us to understand the benefits of some of these systems, whether they were in production, logistics, personnel or whatever. We understood, of course, that this practice is also a double-edged sword.

"While this would supply us with a variety of new ideas, it would be more difficult to assimilate these people into an effective team. We wanted different ideas and suggestions and we knew that these might be controversial. Everybody thinks they have the best way to do something, especially people coming from successful companies. There have been some very animated discussions about all kinds of technical issues—how to assemble a car, whether to

A Helmut Nagel, one of 70 German trainers who will be living in Alabama for up to two years, assists a trainee on an early trial vehicle. **B** The preliminary group of American trainees, in Germany. **C** Assembly techniques are demonstrated on a body-in-white. **D** A team member spot-welds the structure of an M-Class. **E** Team members and executives wear the same informal clothes, and share dining facilities.

do it in an automated way with robotics or manually, how many weld spots go in a car…but we do argue as a team."

Hiring of the production and maintenance team members was a different situation, and the competition for spots at Mercedes was tough. In all, some 45,000 applications were received for these jobs.

The ultimate employment goal for Mercedes in Tuscaloosa is around 1500, with a majority from the state of Alabama and a small number of Germans who will rotate between countries. There will be a continuing German presence because Tuscaloosa is a learning field, with new ideas, processes and procedures that need to be shared with Germany.

From the beginning Mercedes was sensitive to the hiring of minorities. Meyer explains: "One of the key points made early in the process was that we were going to hire people in a proportion—to the extent that we could—that reflects the population of the area. And we've done very well in that regard." Meyer and others from Mercedes met with the Alabama Black Caucus to lay out their plans and objectives and demonstrate a commitment to cultural diversity.

"Our objective," says Meyer, "is to set an example of what can be achieved if you work hard and include people from multiple racial backgrounds. So far, we've done well."

Inevitably, there was the matter of whether the Mercedes factory would be unionized. Meyer explains the company's position. "Our basic objective is to treat people in a positive way—to provide good working conditions and a level of compensation that is competitive within the automotive industry. We have open communications, we deal directly with people, we have an open-office concept,

He swings the steering wheel hard right, the ML320 prototype's tires sing in protest. James Phillips smiles. We're on the long banked turn of the test track at Mercedes' Tuscaloosa factory, and Phillips is hard at work. Then he plants his foot on the accelerator as the track straightens out, letting the M-Class run free as the speed climbs. James Phillips is a happy man.

He's part of the testing department at Tuscaloosa.

And as production gets into full swing, this department will drive samples—about three percent—of the new sport-utility vehicles some 3-4 miles on the test track behind the factory. From the perspective of the customers, Phillips and other testers will hear, feel or sense anything that isn't quite right about the M-Class. Then it will be fixed and its root cause found and eliminated.

Sounds like sweet work for a man who grins easily and says, "I've always been a car enthusiast and Mercedes makes one of the finest products in the world. Therefore, working for Mercedes is not only fun, it's a privilege."

Phillips, 36, who grew up in Battle Creek, Michigan, attended high school and studied automotive technology at the local community college. Also an aviation enthusiast—he has his private pilot's license and has done some skydiving—James went to work as a civil service aircraft technician for the Air Force, and joined the Air National Guard. His wife, Debra, is from Alabama, and they have two sons, William, 3, and Wesley, 18 months. When they heard about Mercedes opening a factory in Tuscaloosa, James figured it sounded like the right place to settle.

Like other job applicants, he found it wasn't easy to get a spot at Mercedes. "It took me a year and about seven tests," Phillips remembers, adding that Mercedes was looking for team-oriented people, a trait he acquired during his military service.

"I look forward to coming to work," says Phillips. "This is a great company, where people aren't robots or clones, but are all thinking along the same lines. We're thinking quality and customer satisfaction. I've worked places were a few people were dragging everyone down. Here everyone is helping each other out."

With that last comment, Phillips smiles and then takes the ML320 back out onto the banking for another test lap.

we don't have reserved parking, and we have an open cafeteria...all those things. This is best for business. In surroundings like that, most people are not disposed to seek union representation. In the end, of course, it's not our decision. It's the workers' right under all the labor laws of the United States. If they want a union, they have every opportunity to seek union representation, have a vote, and decide the issue for themselves."

Those who apply for work at Mercedes will find that the basic requirements aren't that tough, but getting the job is no shoe-in. As Malinda Bean found out when she applied. "I'd never seen a company do this amount of testing before you can get a job," says Bean, who adds that the experience made her feel better about the position and the people she works with. "It proves to me that they really wanted to work and didn't just drive up and apply."

A single mom of a young boy, Bean had to move 150 miles away from her family to work in the raw materials lab at the Mercedes factory, but she says she enjoys getting up in the morning and going to work. Bean likes the fact that everyone, including Andreas Renschler and the team members on the assembly line, wear the same uniforms of knit shirts, sweat shirts and slacks. "It makes you feel a lot more comfortable and the bosses more approachable. No matter how friendly your plant manager is, if you are in grungy clothes and he's in his office behind his desk wearing a suit and tie, you don't feel like you should be in there talking with him. My boss is very open, a nice guy, and I think the fact we're all dressed the same really helps."

In a testament to the significance of the Tuscaloosa plant, 70 German trainers came to Alabama for up to two years from Sindelfingen, the flagship factory where the first American workers trained on the line for six months.

Dieter Gack and Dieter Schmid are just two of the German trainers doing 20-month stints in Tuscaloosa. They admit to missing the food of their homeland, but they have enjoyed the time in Alabama. They love traveling in the U.S.—Schmid had already logged 30,000 miles in his automobile—and are impressed with how friendly Americans can be. And how will-

F With spray guns at hand, two of the paint crew are ready for action. **G** Debra Nelson greets members of the Vance Fire Department. **H** A worker is trained in the subtleties of surface preparation... **I** ...as another is schooled in the installation of the wiring harness.

Teamwork is an important word within the Mercedes-Benz M-Class project, with team members and team leaders alike. But when it comes to the development program of the M-Class, Dr. Gerhard Fritz must be considered the team's coach. A head coach, but not in the fiery image of Vince Lombardi. No, Fritz is more like Tom Landry...the former Dallas Cowboys coach who was a bit calmer but had an equally strong deter-

mination to win. And he has the impressive physical dimensions of a football player himself.

That Fritz's doctoral thesis dealt with the dynamic behavior of tires and roadholding can't hurt the M-Class. After a stint teaching car design, he joined Mercedes in 1978, where he worked with commercial vehicles, and delved into roadholding, testing, mathematical models and brakes. Dr. Fritz moved to the G-Wagen team in 1987, and when that Mercedes 4-wheel-drive vehicle underwent a major reworking he was transferred from the commercial vehicle group to the passenger car division.

Gerhard Fritz, 52, is married and has two daughters. His automotive enthusiasm is boundless, especially the

thrill of driving the most challenging roads. Fritz will set aside an entire day to relax with his favorite hobby of driving fast. Rising early on a Sunday, he can easily spend the entire day driving quickly along the marvelous roads of southern Germany, eastern France and a corner of Switzerland, returning refreshed late in the day.

On the job, Gerhard considers himself lucky to be one of those engineers given a clean sheet of paper and the rare opportunity to create an entirely new vehicle, the M-Class. Better yet, he was provided with a small crew that mixed veterans from the passenger car and the commercial vehicle divisions, thus getting both perspectives.

It also helps, he explains, that, "This is a small team, so we can

make decisions very quickly and thus make progress in a short time. It's better when the people working at the front are able to make major decisions, because they understand the conditions better than someone who is far away from the action."

But was it difficult for a veteran Mercedes engineer to keep up with corporate change of direction over the past five years? Dr. Fritz shrugs the question off, explaining, "It is basically not difficult for an engineer to change. After all, an engineer is trained to look for new methods and solutions. You must only give him the right targets."

The new M-Class makes it clear that Gerhard Fritz and his team have had great success hitting their targets over the past four years.

ing the U.S. Mercedes employees are to learn their new jobs. As production of the first run of non-prototype M-Classes was about to begin, Dieter Gack commented, "The people here are ready."

That includes Randy Harris from the pre-production shop, who recalls, "I was attracted by the name Mercedes-Benz. And I thought it would be a very interesting job. It was difficult to get. It required a lot of

dedication, because there were several tests involved. I think it took a total of close to 60 hours of interviews, tests and training before I even began to be considered."

All the work however, was worth it, because Harris was chosen as one of the first 19 Americans to be sent to Germany.

"We trained at Sindelfingen," Harris explains, "on the assembly line. I worked in the body department and learned

everything about building the body, from the point where the subassemblies are put together up to completed doors ready to ship to paint."

The Americans worked closely with the Germans, who were eager to help. And despite the language difference, Harris notes that they had little trouble communicating. His trainers, Thomas Stradinger and Armin Koch, proved very helpful. On weekends, the Germans would even invite the Americans to their homes for a chance to relax. When Harris' wife, Lori, visited him, they turned their vacation into a second honeymoon.

What did Harris learn in Germany?

"I had worked with metal before," he says, "but they taught me a lot more, the finer points. I look at cars differently now, and whenever I see a new car I immediately begin to look at the contours, how the body fits together, that sort of thing.

"We learned a lot about the company's culture and the Mercedes-Benz philosophy about building the body, and that everything has to be exactly right. We understood what is acceptable or unacceptable when it comes to things like the surface finish or a spot weld. If it's unacceptable, they work it until it's right.

"You come to be conscious of what you're giving to the next guy, because if you give him a part, or whatever it is you're doing, and it's poor quality, then he can't do his job. What you do directly affects the next person. They taught us to really take a lot of pride in what we do."

William Taylor, vice president of operations, says that hiring team members unskilled in automobile production to build the new M-Class in Tuscaloosa remains controversial. Some of Taylor's German colleagues have even expressed amazement that the men and women who will assemble the sport-utility vehicle have so little automotive experience.

But Taylor smiles as he recalls when the first Americans got to Germany and started training. "The first thing that happened," says Taylor, "was that the trainers had to work late at night to make new plans, because the American team members were learning their tasks faster than they could be written. Now the same thing is happening here in Tuscaloosa. When team members join, I like to tell them: 'We're good people here, we've set high standards. You're going to have to meet them or exceed them.' And you know what? They do. They're challenging the daylights out of the parent organization, which is great, because it keeps the spark going and the adrenaline flowing."

J A body shop team member preps an M-Class body that's headed for the paint shop.
K Team members gather to celebrate the start of the first production trial in May, 1996.

A WORLD-CLASS PERFORMER

In a world increasingly filled with sport-utility vehicles, the M-Class had to be different. Most important, it also had to be fit to wear the three-pointed star.

It's a new look, the three-pointed Mercedes-Benz star on the M-Class. But all the right Mercedes styling cues are present, so there is no mistaking the vehicle's heritage. Still, the proportions are out of the ordinary for a Mercedes. Sure, we're used to seeing this sort of overall height, ground clearance and stance with the G-Wagen, which has square corners, flat glass and a utilitarian demeanor. The stylish shape of the M-Class, however, is different, one that hints at other SUVs but is both distinctive and handsome.

There are also numerous mechanical distinctions in the M-Class. Its standard 18-valve V-6 engine, with 215 bhp from 3.2 liters, is the most sophisticated powerplant currently installed in a sport-utility vehicle (and a similar 4.3-liter V-8 follows later). Off-roaders will certainly appreciate the dual-inlet air intake that allows the Mercedes to ford deep water. Moreover, the M-Class is the only SUV with a 5-speed automatic transmission that "learns" the driver's habits and electronically tailors the shift schedule to that style.

Although the M-Class has a center differential that is conventional—in normal conditions it splits the power 50/50 front-to-rear—it is part of a very unusual 4-wheel-drive system called 4ETS. Using open differentials in the transfer case and front and rear axles, the 4ETS system will automatically apply the brakes to a spinning wheel (or wheels), which means that torque, through differential action, will be sent to the wheel (or wheels) with traction. The diagonally split 4-wheel disc brakes are augmented by a 4-channel anti-lock system that has a special low-range program for loose, off-road conditions.

Although many SUVs have independent front suspension, all Mercedes' competitors have a live rear axle. The M-Class

breaks new ground with an independent rear suspension that enhances ride and handling both on- and off-road.

This suspension and driveline have been shown clearly in earlier chapters. But most important, what makes the Mercedes-Benz M-Class feel different than other sport-utility vehicles?

It begins with the "package." This term generally is used to describe how the inside of a vehicle is laid out, and how its interior space is used for both seating and cargo-carrying capacity.

Measured from nose to tail, the M-Class is 180.6 in. long, whereas the Ford Explorer, the best-selling sport-utility vehicle in the world, measures 188.5. The other crucial measurement is wheelbase,

the distance between the front and rear axles. Here, the Mercedes is 111.0 in., just a half-inch shorter than the Explorer. This similarity in wheelbases, contrasted with the difference in overall lengths, means the Mercedes has its wheels set closer to the ends of the vehicle. This is good for several reasons, the two most important being potentially better interior room and shorter front and rear overhangs.

Otherwise, the Mercedes is a bit larger than the Ford, 2.4 in. taller and an inch wider. These measurements translate into an M-Class interior package that's equal in size to the Ford's, even though the Mercedes M-Class is 7.9-in. shorter overall. While front headroom of the M-Class is the same as that of the Explorer, the

M-Class offers nearly a half-inch more rear headroom. The Mercedes also offers its rear occupants 0.8 in. more shoulder room. With the rear seatbacks folded down, the cargo area of the M-Class measures 72.4 in. in length—enough for two adults to sleep back there. With that second row of seatbacks folded, the Mercedes boasts 85.4 cu. ft. of cargo space, versus the Ford's 81.6.

Seating is an important part of the package, of course, and here the M-Class also shines. Front seat accommodations are quite spacious, and there's still sufficient legroom in back for three six-footers. That rear bench seat is divided into three individual sections, each with its own folding seatback and headrest. Three people abreast will be reasonably comfortable, while two passengers in the rear will be in the lap of luxury. And they can fold down the middle seatback to create a convenient table.

While the second seat is configured so that all three seatbacks can fold forward, the bottom cushion has only two pieces. The seat directly behind the front-seat passenger folds forward completely to facilitate access to the cargo area of the M-Class. Although the remaining two seatbacks can be folded forward to add cargo space, their mutual seat cushion does not fold.

In a unique SUV feature, the second-row seats of the M-Class can be moved ahead 3.1 in. for a bit more rear cargo room. The small floor indentation that's

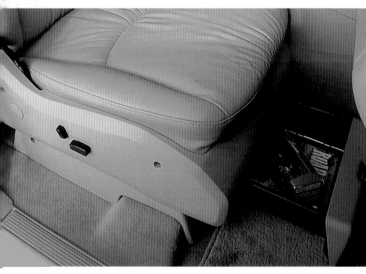

revealed when the seat is moved serves a unique purpose: If the optional third row seat has been ordered, the indentation becomes a foot well for the rearmost passengers. That third row consists of a pair of seats that fold up to the sides of the M-Class interior when not in use. These seats, available within a year after the Mercedes SUV's introduction—complete with D-pillar-mounted shoulder safety belts—can be retrofitted into M-Classes.

Access to the rear cargo area of the M-Class is easy, thanks to the large hatch and a liftover height of 28 in. What's more, the rear hatch opens to a height of 6 ft. 5 in., so there's little danger of most people hitting it with their head. Included in the rear compartment are tie-down points to help keep cargo in place and a first-aid kit in one wheelwell housing. The other housing will hold the optional swing-out Bose CD changer. Outside, under the rear load floor, is a space-saver spare tire. Or you can opt for a rear-mounted full-size spare with a hard cover; it swings out to allow access to the spacious cargo area.

The M-Class can also handle special items like a bicycle, skis or surfboards with an optional carrying rack. There's also a large luggage box that attaches to the standard-equipment roof rails.

Getting into the M-Class is a bit easier than with other sport utilities, thanks to the independent rear suspension. With no need to put the body atop a live rear axle, as in other SUVs, the step-in height is only 18.0 in., which is several inches lower than some other sport utilities with the same size wheels and tires.

Despite this, the Mercedes still has a tall, "in-command" seating position. Those who have owned a Mercedes will immediately recognize the instrument

panel, and though features such as the climate controls and the AM/FM cassette radio are configured differently than in Mercedes' sedans, there's no confusing their genealogy. The vents, buttons, switches, steering wheel and the shift lever will be familiar, but there are also a few changes. These include stubby steering column stalks and switches for the power windows that are pushed down to lower and pulled up to raise the glass. Other interior features include a center console with storage, reading lamps, four cupholders and an extra 12-volt power outlet for rear-seat passengers.

The standard interior has cloth seats with dash and console accent panels that have a carbon-fiber appearance. An option package includes such extras as leather upholstery with heated, 8-way power front seats, walnut trim, a trip computer, auto-dimming rearview mirror and a lockable safe box under the driver's seat.

Those who know Mercedes will feel at home settling into the driver's seat behind the tilt steering wheel. From the moment you drive away, it's obvious that the engineers knew how to get the feel of the C- or E-Class steering into the M-Class because it has the same smooth, direct-connection feel as the company's passenger cars. In fact, all the things you touch and operate are unmistakably Mercedes.

Almost always, the jiggly ride motions and stiff handling manners of an SUV are attributable to its truck underpinnings. This, however, can't be said about the new M-Class. It rides as smoothly as a conventional Mercedes, and its suspension is designed to handle the toughest terrain. All the information that a C- or E-Class would telegraph comes through in the M-Class. Maneuverability is excellent, whether you're tackling a sharp mountain turn or parallel parking in a crowded city. The short overhangs of the M-Class are of great value in either situation.

Those short overhangs also benefit serious off-roaders, because they increase approach and departure angles. And during off-pavement travel over rough surfaces, the independent suspension allows each

wheel to follow the contours of the ground—eliminating much of the bouncing and pitching of a solid-axle SUV. Moreover, driving with 4ETS will be a breeze when veteran drivers learn that you needn't balance the brake and throttle as with other SUVs. In the M-Class, you simply work the gas pedal, and let the magic begin as it climbs out of holes or crawls over logs.

On the road, the M-Class is also a delight to drive. The ride is exceptionally smooth for an SUV, and the handling characteristics are predictable and reassuring. The new V-6 engine provides ample performance and excellent low-end torque. The 5-speed automatic transmission presents the right gear for every need, and gear changes are smooth and positive. Acceleration rates are brisk and fully competitive in this class.

You also can enjoy the competent overall feel and impressive build quality of the M-Class as you drive it on or off the pavement. The innovative 4ETS system means virtually never having to say "I'm stuck," and it's easy to envision the Mercedes SUV as an all-weather, all-roads, all-conditions safe haven.

The driving position is first-class, with excellent lines of sight in all directions. And there is little of the body roll during cornering that is common with SUVs. This is truly a world-class vehicle that states clearly and confidently that it is every inch a Mercedes-Benz.

Making this all the more remarkable is the roughly $35,000 price that was set early on in the M-Class program, back when the cost accountant was an integral part of the development team. Over the years, Mercedes has set many standards, and the M-Class will undoubtedly continue this tradition.

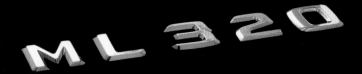

SPECIFICATIONS

Curb weight	4237 lb
Wheelbase	111.0 in.
Track, f/r	60.4 in./60.4 in.
Length	180.6 in.
Width	72.2 in.
Height	69.9 in.
Ground clearance	8.4 in.
Engine type	V-6
Bore x stroke	89.9 mm x 84.0 mm (3.54 in. x 3.31 in.)
Displacement	3199 cc (195.2 cu in.)
Bhp	215 bhp @ 5600 rpm
Torque, lb.-ft.	229 lb-ft @ 3000 rpm
Transmission	5-speed automatic
Suspension, f/r	Independent twin control-arm axle, torsion bars, double-tube gas shocks/ Independent twin control-arm axle, progressive coil springs, double-tube gas shocks
Brakes, f/r	Hydraulic ventilated discs/solid discs w/ 4-channel all-terrain ABS
Steering type	power-assisted rack & pinion
4WD System	AWD system with open center differential and front/rear ETS
Body construction	Body on frame
Side protection	Side guard door beams, side air bags
0–60 mph, sec	9.0
Headroom, f/r	39.8 in./39.7 in.
Shoulder room, f/r	58.3 in./57.9 in.
Cargo capacity, rear seat folded	85.4 cu ft
Cargo area length, rear seat down	72.4 in.
Cargo area height	40.0 in.
Towing capacity	5000 lb
Turning circle	37.0 ft

MOVIE STAR

Mercedes-Benz's M-Class was designed to take on and conquer roads, loose desert sand, muddy trails and snow-packed streets, but angry dinosaurs? Yes indeed. It has a starring role in Steven Spielberg's *The Lost World: Jurassic Park*, **so the company's California design studio made sure the new M-Class was properly equipped for this grand adventure.**

Oscar-winning director Steven Spielberg brought back the prehistoric world and plunked it down on an island in modern times with his smash hit movie, *Jurassic Park*, the largest grossing motion picture in history. Thanks to his cinematic magic, dinosaurs were brought to life and allowed to run free over the island until certain dinosaurs—velociraptors and tyrannosaurus rex—managed to take control and savage a wonderful scientific experiment. Steven Spielberg returns to the same theme of di-

A

nosaurs running free on an island for *The Lost World: Jurassic Park,* his sequel to *Jurassic Park.* In this movie, however, which is produced by Gerald R. Molen and Colin Wilson, the scientists return to the Jurassic Period in Mercedes-Benz M-Class sport-utility vehicles.

Looking for ways to introduce its new M-Class to the public, Mercedes signed on with Universal Studios and Amblin Entertainment to provide vehicles for the new movie. The new M-Class, however, would need to be modified, fitted with all the expedition equipment one might expect of scientists heading into a lost world to search for dinosaurs. The job logically fell to the Mercedes-Benz Advanced Design studio in Irvine, California, about an hour's drive south of the major Hollywood movie lots.

B

Gerhard Steinle, who heads the California studio, began by having any designers interested in the project sketch some possibilities. This was the "ideation" phase in which designers are asked to set their imaginations free with only one require-

A A rendering from the second phase of "ideation," where André Frey toned down Amblin's original concepts to something more recognizable as an M-Class. **B** After sketch A was deemed too timid, this heavily caged dinosaur-chaser was penned. Frey says the look was perceived as "too military, too brutal." **C** The creative forces of Amblin Entertainment and Mercedes-Benz merge: from left to right, Amblin's Warren Manser (production illustrator) and Jim Teegarden (art director) and Mercedes' Melonee Ranzinger, Frey and Gerhard Steinle. **D** Moving closer to final form, Frey's illustration shows the unusual brush guards, air snorkel and perforated rocker panels. **E** Sketch D's roof-top canopy matures into a collapsible tower (sort of the dinosaur equivalent of a shark cage) in this John Bell drawing.

ment: Underneath all the jungle equipment and camouflage, the movie vehicles had to retain the basic M-Class shape and be recognizable.

At the same time, Steven Spielberg had the movie experts at Industrial Light and Magic, and freelance designers, pen their ideas of what *The Lost World:Jurassic Park* vehicles should look like. Remember the famous John Wayne movie, *Hatari*? In that film about capturing wild animals in Africa, Wayne and crew used a sport-utility vehicle with outrigger seats, which

C

D

BRUSHGUARD FOLLOWS HEADLAMP CHARACTHER LINE.

UMBRELLA-LIKE COLLAPSABLE OBSERVATION CAGE

RAISEABLE SEATS TURN 360°

HEAVY-DUTY PROTECTION

12/19/95. APPROVED AAV. # 2.

GATHERERS
MODIFIED M.B. AAV

E

helped inspire the movie studio's approach to the M-Class modifications.

After the first run of design sketches, Steinle assigned André Frey as the project leader for the movie vehicles. Born in Zurich, Switzerland, Frey studied at both the European and American campuses of the Art Center College of Design before going to work for Mercedes. In creating

The Lost World: Jurassic Park designs, Frey explains, "I thought a bit about *Hatari* too, but at the same time I thought about *Jurassic Park*, in which the Ford Explorers were meant more for a joy ride. The M-Class had to be more utilitarian."

With an armload of sketches, Steinle went to Amblin, where everyone's ideas were spread out on the floor of a sound stage for review by Steven Spielberg. While the film production and art designers had wonderfully radical sketches, the look of the Mercedes had been lost. The hunt continued.

More meetings led to other ideas. When the members of the film crew visited the Irvine studio and saw the Swatch SMART car designed in California, they even considered using these tiny cars as vehicles in which the good guys could hide from the bad guys in larger machines. That, however, was considered to be too far off track. It was then decided to use disguised versions of Mercedes Unimogs, the company's industrial 4-wheel-drive workhorses, for the hunters.

Frey developed still more sketches, and finally got down to three that everyone agreed on. Needing a rolling laboratory meant that one of the vehicles was enclosed, while a second featured a dino-spotting tower that rises up from the back of the M-Class. Third was a convertible with just a framework around the four windows and doors...and *does not* hint at future plans for the production sport utility. In addition, Frey had to add all external pieces, such as front bull bars, hang-on jerry cans and protective bars for the side windows. Sums up Steinle: "It wasn't so much a design job as a decoration job. But it was a lot of fun."

Design sketches had to be turned into real, completely functional vehicles. And for this, Mercedes turned to Metalcrafters, a Southern California firm that is quickly becoming a legend among builders of special vehicles. Starting with early production prototypes of the M-Class, the metal benders, welders and other wizards at Metalcrafters needed just three months to convert the vehicles into the finished Mercedes that would take on *The Lost World: Jurassic Park*.

There was one last-minute hiccup. Mercedes couldn't decide on the final camouflage treatment. With just 48 hours left before shooting began, it was decided to redo the paint, but Metalcrafters' paint booths were booked solid. So another member of the Mercedes family came forward. The company's Vehicle Preparation Center in Carson, just a half-hour north of Irvine, opened up its paint facilities to the design studio. The VPC crew began stripping the previous paint schemes and soon

F The movie cars near the end of their three-month conversion at Metalcrafters' shop in Fountain Valley, California. **G** The final cosmetically-correct M-Class mockup, as presented to Amblin Entertainment for approval. **H** This open-top version of the M-Class was created specifically for the movie, and does not mean a convertible version is planned for production.

Frey went to work with a spray gun. There were two copies each of the three vehicles, and the pairs had to be identical. For almost 48 hours straight, Frey and the VPC team stripped and painted. As tough as it was, Frey says, "It was just awesome teamwork. It was a lot of fun to deal with the real vehicles and have a lot of motivated people around… that was the best part."

Just in time, *The Lost World: Jurassic Park* Mercedes M-Class vehicles were in front of the movie cameras, where the film's standby painter, Tony Leonardi, stayed very busy prepping them to take on the celluloid dinosaurs.

The work for Gerhard Steinle and the Advanced Design studio, however, was not over. With the movie exposure came a plan for promoting and merchandising the modified M-Class vehicles used in *The Lost World: Jurassic Park*. So six months before the movie premiere, with toy companies Hasbro and Tyco ready to start producing miniature versions of the movie M-Classes, Gerhard Steinle's desk was crowded with these unique scale models, waiting for his comments. Sitting among the many other models of vintage Mercedes were these rather different micro-M-Class machines, not fitted with the stylish bodywork of the legendary SSK or the gullwing doors of the 300SL, but with the very purposeful cage work and camouflage. It wouldn't have been surprising to see a tiny triceratops charge across his desk!

14 Andreas Renschler, President & CEO, MBUSI

THE M TEAM

After four years with the M-Class project, Andreas Renschler says it would have been impossible to create a trailblazing 4-wheel-drive sport-utility vehicle without teamwork. Here, in his own words, he salutes the entire M-Class team.

Looking back on the life of the M-Class, it's hard to believe how short its history really is. Just four years ago, the M-Class was only a vision. We had an idea, a blank sheet of paper and a belief in creating something exciting and successful. Today, this vision has become a reality. And it was only possible through the hard work, dedication and unwavering enthusiasm of a team of individuals in both Alabama and Germany.

What we have been able to accomplish in this relatively short time has been great—we've developed a new vehicle in just 34 months; simultaneously built a new plant in a new country; and brought together a new team of individuals to

159

build our M-Class All-Activity Vehicle.

It took so many people to make all this possible. Our team spans two continents and includes people from different backgrounds with different experiences. People both new and old to Mercedes-Benz. Yet, each with one goal in mind—to do his or her part to develop and produce the

M-CLASS MILESTONES

Project Start...........................1/93

Direction Decision....................7/93

Design Freeze..........................2/94

Start Testing Pre-Prototypes.........5/94

First Crash Test With Mock-Up......5/94

First Crash Test With Prototype....2/95

First Prototype Function Test........3/95

Start Production Trial 5/96

Completion of Production Trials ...12/96

TOTAL DEVELOPMENT TIME: 34 MONTHS

Mercedes considers actual development time for the M-Class to have begun with the release of the styling model interior in February, 1994. Development ended with the last of the third production trial vehicles in December, 1996, giving the M-Class the short development time of only 34 months.

world's finest sport-utility vehicle.

The members of our development team, primarily based in Stuttgart, led the way by using their relentless attention to quality, safety and innovation to create a vehicle which would set a new standard among sport utilities.

Our young team in Tuscaloosa has, in just a short time, mastered the Mercedes tradition of building the highest quality products in the world. This hasn't always been easy, with many long hours away from their families. In fact, many of our team members spent months overseas training at our Sindelfingen factory. They were led and continue to be supported by some of the finest trainers from our plants in Germany. This support will play a key role in helping us build the highest quality vehicle for our customers.

There are so many others who helped make the M-Class possible. Our suppliers, who have been our partners from development through production of the M-Class, and who will help us achieve our high quality standards. Our marketing and sales companies throughout the world, that kept us focused on the needs and wants of our customers. And, of course, our many colleagues throughout the Daimler-Benz organization who not only supported us with resources and expertise, but also encouraged us to push the envelope and achieve things never tried before.

And I cannot forget the people of Alabama. They not only helped us as we established our business in the state, but also warmly welcomed us as neighbors and friends. We are so happy to call Alabama our home.

A world-class team of people has made the Mercedes-Benz M-Class a world-class product. It has been my honor to be a part of this wonderful team!

build our M-Class All-Activity Vehicle.

It took so many people to make all this possible. Our team spans two continents and includes people from different backgrounds with different experiences. People both new and old to Mercedes-Benz. Yet, each with one goal in mind—to do his or her part to develop and produce the world's finest sport-utility vehicle.

The members of our development team, primarily based in Stuttgart, led the way by using their relentless attention to quality, safety and innovation to create a vehicle which would set a new standard among sport utilities.

Our young team in Tuscaloosa has, in just a short time, mastered the Mercedes tradition of building the highest quality products in the world. This hasn't always been easy, with many long hours away from their families. In fact, many of our team members spent months overseas training at our Sindelfingen factory. They were led and continue to be supported by some of the finest trainers from our plants in Germany. This support will play a key role in helping us build the highest quality vehicle for our customers.

There are so many others who helped make the M-Class possible. Our suppliers, who have been our partners from development through production of the M-Class, and who will help us achieve our high quality standards. Our marketing and sales companies throughout the world, that kept us focused on the needs and wants of our customers. And, of course, our many colleagues throughout the Daimler-Benz organization who not only supported us with resources and expertise, but also encouraged us to push the envelope and achieve things never tried before.

And I cannot forget the people of Alabama. They not only helped us as we established our business in the state, but also warmly welcomed us as neighbors and friends. We are so happy to call Alabama our home.

A world-class team of people has made the Mercedes-Benz M-Class a world-class product. It has been my honor to be a part of this wonderful team!

M-CLASS MILESTONES

Project Start...1/93

Direction Decision............................7/93

Design Freeze....................................2/94

Start Testing Pre-Prototypes..........5/94

First Crash Test With Mock-Up.......5/94

First Crash Test With Prototype....2/95

First Prototype Function Test.........3/95

Start Production Trial 5/96

Completion of Production Trials ...12/96

TOTAL DEVELOPMENT TIME: 34 MONTHS

Mercedes considers actual development time for the M-Class to have begun with the release of the styling model interior in February, 1994. Development ended with the last of the third production trial vehicles in December, 1996, giving the M-Class the short development time of only 34 months.